THE HIDDEN TREASURES IN

Philippians

AN
INDUCTIVE
BIBLE STUDY
BY
EVELYN
WHEELER

LIBERTY
BOOKS

P.O. Box 23537, Richfield, MN 55423

Truth Trackers: The Hidden Treasures in Philippians
Copyright © 1999 by Evelyn Wheeler
Published by Liberty Books
P.O. Box 23537
Richfield, Minnesota 55423

ISBN 1-886930-25-2

Printed in the United States of America.

02 03 04 05 06 / 10 9 8 7 6 5 4 3 2

To my parents

who always gave me every opportunity to learn and grow.

Acknowledgments

Two friends encouraged me toward this project: Kay Zahasky who believed I was to write Bible studies for children and who prodded me toward it. Eileen Mason who opened the opportunity, walked through the process with me, and pushed me on when I wanted to quit.

Contents

Hidden Treasures of the Bible

Welcome to a study of the book of Philippians. You're joining a great group of kids called Truth Trackers!

Our study is like a great archaeological dig! Archaeologists are people who dig through remains of old civilizations to understand how men, women, and children lived thousands of years ago. As they piece together the bits of the past that they discover, they eventually get a bigger picture of what life was like.

Like archaeologists, we are going to dig below the surface of the book of Philippians and discover many truths and treasures. Together we're going to dig and sift and sort through this book so that you come away with truths that will help you for the rest of your life. Yes, the great thing about the dig you'll be on is that the "finds" you unearth can change your life! As you put these together, you'll get a bigger picture too—a picture of what God is saying to you about some key issues.

Before you start, meet a friendly camel named Clayton. His ancestors lived in Bible times, so he has heard all of the stories of the Bible as they have been passed down from generation to generation. He even had a distant uncle in Bethlehem the night Jesus was born. Clayton will be the head archaeologist on this exciting adventure! He'll talk you through each dig.

As you begin this incredible dig on the book of Philippians, remember that archaeologists work very hard, long hours. They have very exciting jobs, and the result of their work is very rewarding. Remember, too, that you can't unearth the treasures that unlock keys to past civilizations without lots of work!

So as you begin, think about the fact that you won't discover the kind of truths we are after sitting in front of the television or at your computer. You have to get up, grab your boots, hat, tools, and dig into the Word. You have to push through all five layers of each dig to understand all of what God wants to say to you. It won't happen if you don't get up, dig in, and do your part.

There will be many, many times throughout your life that you'll be glad you spent this time digging in the Bible because you'll know what God says and what He wants. And then you'll be able to do the right thing and please Him! You'll have a treasure chest full of truth that will help you all of your life!

We're almost ready to get started digging. First let me tell you some "rules of the road, " as they say.

Tools of the Trade: At the first of each lesson is a list of tools you'll need to do the lesson. You should always gather these together before you begin. Like a good archaeologist, you need the right tools to get the job done.

Directions for Diggers: This short section is the introduction to each lesson and gives you an idea of the dig's topic. On any dig, there is a head archaeologist who directs the dig, so Clayton will talk you through this brief section.

Chart the Course: You'll have a chance to work on maps and charts that will help you understand the material. At a dig site, there is a graph or map that shows the team where to dig. These maps and charts in your study will point the way to truth treasures for you! Whenever you see a map, be sure you look at it to find the locations mentioned in the work you're doing that day!

Clues: As you work though the digs, from time to time you'll be given clues that will help you unearth truth. Every site has clues that point to where special treasures can be discovered. You'll be given clues to point you to truth as you work.

Treasure Map: It is easier to find treasures if you have a master map of the area where you're working. The book of Philippians is your master map for this dig. It is called the "Treasure Map" because through the study of it, you'll discover GREAT treasures. It is printed at the back of your study book.

 Checking in with Headquarters: Each time you begin a new dig, you should pray and ask the Holy Spirit to teach you truth. Just like on a dig when everyone checks in with the head guy for directions for the day, you should check in for help with your study.

Special Find: On digs, there are times when very special artifacts are uncovered. In fact, Clayton was on a dig recently when a water jug was unearthed—and it was all in one piece. This is a very special find because most of the time, bits and pieces of treasures are pulled out and have to be pieced together later. These little sections will help you find very special truths!

Truth Treasures for the Week: At the end of each week's dig, you'll see a place for you to record three truth treasures you discovered. On an archaeological dig, when a section of the dig is complete, all of the finds are tagged and information about each is noted. In the same way, you'll tag some key truths and note them. Be sure not to skip this section! You're on your own when it comes to this part, but it is *very* important.

Bury the Treasure: One of the wisest things you can do is to memorize the Word of God. Each dig has a special treasure that you'll unearth, and you'll want to bury it in your heart.

Puzzles: Throughout the study, you'll find a variety of fun puzzles that will help you review the truth you're learning. It is kind of like being on a dig and watching as the head archaeologist tries to piece parts of the finds together to see if they have discovered a table, a jar, a bowl, or who knows what! It'll be fun to work through these and see what you discover! (A key to each puzzle can be found at the back of the book so that you can check your answers.)

**Well, you're prepared. Are you ready?
I hope so. Take off to Dig One. Clayton will meet you there.**

Dig 1

Our Adventure Begins!

Tools of the Trade

1. Colored pencils
2. Pen or pencil
3. Treasure Map of the book of Philippians on pages 155-160
4. Chart: A Look At Philippians on page 15
5. People Puzzle on page 16

Directions for Diggers

Has your mom ever asked you to take out the trash or pick up your room while you're watching your favorite TV program? Did you stop right away, or did you ignore your mother until the program was over?

Has a brother, a sister, or a friend ever lost or broken something that was special to you? What did you do?

How do you feel when your friend asks you to go to a ball game or a movie and your dad tells you that he has some chores you have to do instead?

Our study in Philippians will help you know how God wants you to react—even when you're in difficult situations like these. When you know what God says, you can always decide to do what would please Him.

9

You'll also learn how and why you can still be joyful even when things don't go your way! You'll see that there is a reason to rejoice, or be happy, in all things—even in things that you don't like or that you don't really think are fair.

God wants to teach you to walk through life with Him. He wants you to become a young person who loves Him. If you'll study hard and practice the things that you learn, you'll be excited to see how God can work in your life—and you'll be excited to see how He can use you to help other boys and girls know Him too!

Let's get started in our study. You'll see that studying the Bible can be a lot of fun. It may seem like a lot of work sometimes too, but don't give up. Ask God to help you to be the best student you can be.

And here's a clue to help you get off to a great start: **Clue #1:** It will be much easier if you work on each dig one layer at a time. Just dig through one layer each day instead of trying to work through an entire dig at once.

LAYER ONE: Checking in With Headquarters

1. Do you know who helps us understand the Word of God? It is the Holy Spirit. He is our teacher when it comes to the Word of God. So when you study the Bible, you need to ask Him to help you understand what God is telling you in His Word.

John 16:13 says this: "But when He, the Spirit of truth, comes, He will guide you into all the truth…." This verse is a promise that the Holy Spirit will help you understand the truth that God has put in the Bible.

You can think of it this way: When you have a problem in school, you raise your hand to ask the teacher for help. The teacher comes to your desk and helps you with your question. When you pray, asking the Holy Spirit for help, it is like being in the classroom and asking the teacher a question.

So if you get stuck or if you can't seem to understand a part of this lesson, you can pray. God doesn't want you to be left in the dark. He wants you to be in the light. He is never too busy to help. He might show you the answer right away, or He might show you the answer later. But He will show you.

Remember that we call prayer "checking in with headquarters." You should check in each day before you start your digging! You wouldn't start on an important archeological dig without checking with the boss for instructions and help. We don't want to dig into God's Word without asking for the help of the Holy Spirit, our Teacher and Guide!

2. Have you ever flown in an airplane? When you're high off the ground, you can see a whole city. Even though you can't see the details like the street signs, the traffic lights, or the color of the buildings, you can get an idea of what the city and the area around it are like.

That's what we'll be doing this week as we look at the whole book of Philippians. It will be like flying over God's Word in a plane. We'll see the big picture. Later we'll land and look at the street signs, traffic lights, and buildings. That means we'll look at the details of each chapter and the verses in each one to see what they mean.

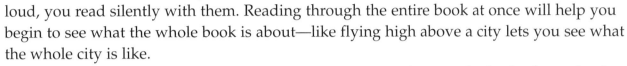

Here we go. Are you ready? Your assignment for today is to read the whole book of Philippians. Don't let that scare you. You'll have some help!

As you read Philippians, ask one of your parents, an older brother or sister, or an older friend to read it out loud to you. While they read it out loud, you read silently with them. Reading through the entire book at once will help you begin to see what the whole book is about—like flying high above a city lets you see what the whole city is like.

Remember that the entire book of Philippians is printed out in the back of your book on pages 155-160. This printout is your "Treasure Map" to truth! Turn to this section and read through the book of Philippians—all four chapters.

Don't worry if you don't understand everything. Just keep reading! Have you ever heard people say that you must begin at the beginning? Well, in the case of this study, that is a good saying for us. Where is the beginning? The beginning is to read the book of Philippians all the way from chapter 1 through chapter 4. Taking time to read the book will help you begin to understand what it all means.

So read the book of Philippians out loud! After you finish the WHOLE book, you're all done for today.

**I am proud of you. You have done well.
I'll look forward to seeing you when you begin digging on Layer Two!**

LAYER TWO: The Big Picture

Yesterday you read through the book of Philippians and got an idea of what the whole book is about. The book of Philippians isn't a very long book, is it? It is about as long as a good letter. As a matter of fact, these four chapters are called an "epistle"—which really means a letter. What you're studying is a letter to a group of people who lived in the city of Philippi.

Since you've read this entire letter once, let's land the plane, get out, grab our picks and dig around for a closer look—one chapter at a time.

1. Again turn to your "Treasure Map" in the back of the book where Philippians is printed out for you on pages 155-160 and read through Philippians 1. This time you'll be reading it yourself. If you read out loud, you'll remember it better.

2. Now, find the chart at the end of this lesson on page 15 so you can "chart the course." Look at the chart and find the column called "Chapter Titles." In that column are two possible titles for chapter 1. Think back over what you read in chapter one and circle the title you think is the best one for the chapter.

Clue #2: Your chapter title should tell you what the author talks about the most in that chapter. It should also help you remember what the chapter says.

3. Do you like to draw? I do! Now you get to be an artist! If you don't have your colored pencils, run grab them! You're going to do an illustration!

An illustration is a picture used to explain something. Story books and comic books use lots of illustrations. The artist draws a picture to show your eyes the meaning of the words that you're reading. As you can see, there are illustrations of me, Clayton the Camel, all through this Bible study book! You can call me Clay for short!

It's lots of fun to draw illustrations! Ready? Go back to the chart on page 15. In the column called "Illustrations" beside the title of chapter 1, draw what you think is the main happening in chapter 1. You don't have to draw everything, just draw the main event of the chapter.

Have fun, and I'll see you when we dig into Layer Three!

LAYER THREE: Tracking the Treasure

Well, it's another day for us to dig together in the book of Philippians. Remember the time you're spending in this study will help you live a life that pleases God if you love Him and decide to do what He says!

1. What does any good student of the Word of God do before beginning their study? If you said "pray," you're right! So take a moment and check in with headquarters. Ask the Holy Spirit to help you understand what God is saying to you in His Word.

2. Now turn to the "Treasure Map" at the back of the book on pages 155-160 and read through Philippians chapter 2. As you read, remember to think about what this chapter talks about the most. That will help you to choose a title and draw a great illustration!

3. I want you to be an artist again today! Do exactly what you did yesterday when you worked on the chart at the end of the lesson—only this time work on chapter 2. Decide on your title and draw your illustration.

Enjoy your study time. Catch you tomorrow.

LAYER FOUR: Picking Through to the Treasures

1. Are you having fun? Take out your pick again today and dig through chapter 3. Don't forget to think about the main points of the chapter as you read.

2. Do you have your colored pencils ready? Continue to "chart the course" by choosing your title for the chapter and by drawing your illustration.

Good job! Take a cool break after a hot day of digging.
Meet you at Layer Five tomorrow!

LAYER FIVE: An A-1 Bible Student

Today you'll dig into the last chapter of this letter you're studying. I am excited that you've made it to this point. Hope you are excited about some of the treasures you're discovering! You're doing great!

1. Read Philippians chapter 4 and think about the main topic.

2. "Chart the course" now for chapter 4.

3. Now that you've finished digging, on the next page write the truth treasures you've discovered in this dig. And don't forget to "Bury the Treasure." This is a verse from another book of the Bible that encourages us to study God's Word. This is a great verse to bury in your heart as we start our study together. You'll get used to ending each dig this way.

Well, my friend, you've done an amazing job on Dig One! Are you excited about the fact that YOU are mining out the truth of this book for yourself?

You should be excited! God will use what you're learning as you grow up to make you into a person who pleases Him in all you do!

Take a moment and thank the Holy Spirit for helping you understand truth. Tell Him you want to understand more as you continue in this study next week.

You're on your way to becoming an "A-1" Bible student. Thanks for hanging in there. You won't be sorry!

See you at the next dig!

PS: For a real adventure, try your hand at digging through the "People Puzzle" on page 16.

Truth Treasures for the Week

1.

2.

3.

Bury the Treasure:

Be diligent to present yourself approved to God as a workman who does not need to be ashamed, accurately handling the word of truth (2 Timothy 2:15).

CLUE #3: Here the word of truth is the same as the Word of God. To accurately handle the Word, you need to study it and understand it. Then you can handle it well.

A Look at Philippians

Chapter Title	Illustrations

Chapter 1

Paul shares Christ in prison

Paul writes to and prays
for the Philippian church

Chapter 2

We should be a servant like
Jesus was a servant

God is working in our lives

Chapter 3

Knowing Christ is
more important than things

Moving closer to Christ

Chapter 4

The Lord can help you rejoice

You should pray instead of worry

People Puzzle

1 The names of eight people mentioned in the book of Philippians are hidden in the puzzle under the heading "Hidden Names."

2 To solve the puzzle, look through the book of Philippians on your "Treasure Map" and color any person's name with the tool of your blue pencil.

3 Now look back through to see where you have colored names blue and record the names on a separate piece of paper.

4 Now using your list as a guide, look at each line of the puzzle and see if you can unscramble the hidden name.

5 Once you have all of the names unscrambled, look at each line and find the letter inside the (parenthesis). Take each of these letters and fill in the line of (parentheses) under the heading "New Scramble Name."

6 Now, see if you can unscramble this name on the second line under "New Scramble Name." **Clue #4:** It is a title.

Hidden Names

ULPA   (_) _ _ _

TNEMELC   _ (_) _ _ _ _ _

UDIAEO   _ _ _ _ (_) _

SUTIDPHROEPA _ (_) _ (_) _ _ _ _ _ _ _ _

MOTHYTI   _ (_) _ _ _ (_) _

TYCHESYN   _ _ (_) _ _ _ _ _

JABENMIN   _ _ _ _ _ _ (_) _

CASARE   _ (_) _ (_) _ _

New Scramble Name

(_) (_) (_) (_) (_) (_) (_) (_) (_) (_) (_)

_ _ _ _ _ _ _ _ _ _

16

Dig 2

Paul—A Master Digger

Tools of the Trade

1. Colored pencils
2. Pen or pencil
3. Chart: Paul and the Philippians on page 29
4. Treasure Map of the book of Philippians on pages 155-160
5. Key Word Puzzle on page 30

Directions for Diggers

Do you like to meet new friends? I think it is fun because you get to learn about the things they like to do, about their family, about what foods they like best, about which movies are their favorites, and you get to share about yourself! New friendships can be great!

Well, this week you're going to meet a man I think you'll like. He is the man who wrote the book we are studying. He lived 2,000 years ago, and he was a Master Digger. He didn't start out this way, but he learned to love the truth above all things and he spent his life living it!

In the beginning, however, this man didn't like the truth and he didn't like Christians. In fact, he did everything he could to stop them from believing in Jesus. His name was Saul. Later his name is changed to Paul. You'll be excited to learn why!

LAYER ONE: Looking for Clues

Today, you'll search out answers to some important questions by using the clues I'll give you. You'll dig around in Philippians chapter 1 to see what you can uncover about Paul.

1. You're going to "chart the course" today by working on a chart called "Paul and the Philippians." You'll unearth some important facts about Paul, and you'll find some small treasures about the people he wrote to, the Philippians.

This chart is pretty easy because I ask some questions and you find the answers in Philippians. It won't be too hard because I'll give you some **Clues**. With each question, I've given you the chapter and verse for you to read to find the answer.

Remember the "Treasure Map" of the book of Philippians is printed out at the back of your book on pages 155-160, so it will be easy to use that to find your answers.

Turn to the chart on page 29 at the end of the lesson and "chart the course!" When you finish, go on to question 2.

But first, don't forget to check in with headquarters. Pray!

2. Do you know how they built houses in Israel in Bible times? One stone on top of another! We are building truth into our lives the same way! One stone of truth on top of another! Let's go over the stones of truth you've just unearthed!

Stone 1—Paul and Timothy, who was like Paul's son, called themselves bond-servants. (We will study about what it means to be a bond-servant in a later lesson.)

Stone 2—Paul was in prison when he wrote this letter to his friends. Many believe that he asked Timothy to write down what he wanted to say because Paul's eyesight was not good. It was hard for him to see his writing.

Stone 3—Paul wrote this letter to the church at Philippi. Paul loved them very much, and that was one of the reasons he wrote.

Just look at all that you uncovered from digging out answers to the questions on the chart! You can find out a lot of things about any book of the Bible just by digging through questions.

I am glad you know a little about Paul and about the people he wrote to. We'll discover more as we continue our study.

You're doing so well! I'm glad that you're hanging in there and not giving up. I know you are tired and a little dirty from the dig, so take a break and enjoy a cool glass of lemonade. And keep up the good work!

LAYER TWO: He Hated Christians

For the next few days, we're going to dig out all we can about Paul. We want to dig carefully and sift though the chapter slowly because there are some hidden treasures about his life to discover. Let's make it our goal to learn all we can about this man of God.

We'll also see what we can learn about the people who lived in Philippi.

Remember that Paul was in prison when he wrote to the Philippians. He didn't want them to be upset about his situation. He tells them that being in prison was really working out for good. His goal in life was to know Christ and have others know Him. Because he was in prison, people were teaching more and more about Jesus. This made Paul happy. He was content and full of joy. He was rejoicing.

Can you see why Paul would rejoice? His goal was being reached even though he was sitting in a prison! He was glad about that and not sad about how it was happening!

Let's dig around and see what we can find out about this man who doesn't mind being in prison for the gospel of Jesus Christ! We'll begin in another book of the Bible. In the book of Acts, we can see what Paul was like before he believed in the Lord Jesus Christ as his Savior and Lord.

To make this easier for you, I'll print the verses from Acts that you need to read right on the page. That'll save some digging time!

1. When we meet Paul in the book of Acts, he is called by a different name. He is called Saul. Saul is with many other people who are listening to a young man named Stephen. Stephen is telling people about the mighty works of God.

The people did not like what Stephen told them. It made them realize that they could be living better lives. Instead of asking God to help them, they attacked Stephen. Sometimes people do not like to hear the truth—even though it is what they need to hear.

Let's see what happened to Stephen. Read Acts 7:57-60. Then answer the questions that follow.

57 But they cried out with a loud voice, and covered their ears and rushed at him with one impulse. **58** When they had driven him out of the city, they *began* stoning *him*; and the witnesses laid aside their robes at the feet of the young man named Saul. **59** They went on stoning Stephen as he called on *the Lord* and said, "Lord Jesus, receive my spirit!" **60** Then falling on his knees, he cried out with a loud voice, "Lord, do not hold this sin against them!" Having said this, he fell asleep.

    a. What happened to Stephen? (When you see the words "fell asleep" in the Word of God, most of the time it means that the person being spoken of is dead.)

Stephen had really done nothing wrong, according to the law of that day. He had just told people that they had disobeyed God's law. The people did not want to hear the truth.

    b. Do you know what it means to be stoned? Long ago, stoning was one way that men and women who had not kept the law of the land were put to death. The guilty person would be surrounded by those who were going to put him to death, and they would throw stones at him until he was dead. Wouldn't that be a horrible way to die?

    c. Have you ever been blamed for doing something wrong when you were innocent? Do you sometimes feel embarrassed to stand up for what is right or to tell other kids about Jesus? Remember that some people have stood up for Him even though it meant that they had to die.

Can you learn to stand up for Him in your classroom, on your soccer team, in ballet class, in the lunch room? It won't cost you your life, but it may mean that kids will think you're different. But I am sure they wish that they had enough nerve to stand up for what is right too!

Think about it all, and the next time you have a hard time standing up for the Lord Jesus Christ, ask God to remind you of Stephen.

2. Look back to number 1 and read Acts 7:58 again.
    a. Who is mentioned?

    b. What did his name become later? (If you can't remember, look at question 1.)

3. Now read Acts 8:1 below.

Saul was in hearty agreement with putting him to death. And on that day a great persecution began against the church in Jerusalem, and they were all scattered throughout the regions of Judea and Samaria, except the apostles.

4. What do you learn in Acts 8:1 about Saul? Did he agree with the way the people had killed Stephen?

5. Read Acts 8:3 below.

> But Saul *began* ravaging the church, entering house after house, and dragging off men and women, he would put them in prison.

6. What did Saul begin to do to those who loved the Lord Jesus (referred to as the "church" in the verse above)?

7. Read Acts 9:1-2.

> **1** Now Saul, still breathing threats and murder against the disciples of the Lord, went to the high priest, **2** and asked for letters from him to the synagogues at Damascus, so that if he found any belonging to the Way, both men and women, he might bring them bound to Jerusalem.

8. Why did Saul ask for the letter from the high priest? ("The Way" is what Christians were called. When you see the words "bring them bound to Jerusalem," it means that he wanted to put them in prison.)

It's hard to believe that the Paul who wrote the book of Philippians is the same man we are reading about in Acts, isn't it?

Tomorrow we'll discover how Saul, the hater of Christians, became Paul, the man who loved the Lord with his whole heart.

LAYER THREE: Saul Sees Jesus

Today we'll continue to dig around in the book of Acts. We want to see what happened to turn Saul into Paul. He changed so much!

Remember, Saul was the man who hated the Way—believers in the Lord Jesus Christ. But he became Paul, the man who loved Jesus so much that he would go to prison before he would stop telling people about Jesus!

We'll read and talk about a few verses at a time so that we don't have too much to read at once! Ready? Let's go!

1. Read Acts 9:3-9. Then answer the questions that follow.

> **3** As he [Saul] was traveling, it happened that he was approaching Damascus, and suddenly a light from heaven flashed around him; **4** and he fell to the ground and heard a voice saying to him, "Saul, Saul, why are you persecuting Me?" **5** And he said, "Who are You, Lord?" And He *said*, "I am Jesus whom you are persecuting, **6** but get up and enter the city, and it will be told you what you must do." **7** The men who traveled with him stood speechless,

hearing the voice but seeing no one. ⁸ Saul got up from the ground, and though his eyes were open, he could see nothing; and leading him by the hand, they brought him into Damascus. ⁹ And he was three days without sight, and neither ate nor drank.

a. You may want to go back and read verses 1-2 from yesterday in number 7 again so that you remember how this chapter begins.

b. What happened to Saul on the road to Damascus? Try this Lipogram to find the answer. (A Lipogram is writing that avoids the use of particular letters. For example: ch _ _ ch. You would fill in the blanks with "u" and "r" to make the word "church.") Solving this Lipogram will help us move through the story and not miss anything!

(1) Suddenly a li _ _ t from h _ _ ven flashed around him; (v. 3)
(2) he fe _ _ to the ground, (v. 4)
(3) and heard a v _ _ ce saying to him, "S _ _ l, S _ _ l, w _ _ are you per _ _ cut _ ng Me?" (v. 4)
(Congratulations, on finishing your first Lipogram!)

c. What was Saul's reaction? What did he say when he heard the voice?

d. What was the answer he received back?

e. Jesus was already dead, buried, raised and in heaven, so why did Jesus say that Saul was persecuting Him? Let's think this one through together. Answer this question first: Who was Saul persecuting? You should know the answer from what we have studied.

Do you think Jesus was saying that because Saul was persecuting the Christians, he was also persecuting Jesus? Isn't it neat to think that Jesus loves you so much that He would say He was being persecuted if you are being persecuted?

The next time someone hurts you, remember that Jesus loves you so much that it hurts Him too. When things like this happen, always talk to Him about it. He understands how you feel, and He wants you to know that He loves you and is concerned about you.

2. Read Acts 9:8-9 again. Look back at number 1 to find the verses.

    a.   What happened to Saul?

    b.   How long was he in this condition?

    c.   Where did they take Saul?

Tomorrow we'll pick back up with the story of Saul and dig into it some more. Today why don't you thank the Lord that He can save anyone! He even saved a man who hated Him and killed Christians!

Layer Four: A New Name

You'll remember from yesterday that some men took Saul into Damascus. These men had been traveling with Saul when he saw the light and heard Jesus' voice.

Let's pick back up with our story and see what happened to Saul.

1. Read Acts 9:10-12 and answer the questions that follow.

10 Now there was a disciple at Damascus named Ananias; and the Lord said to him in a vision, "Ananias." And he said, "Here I am, Lord." **11** And the Lord *said* to him, "Get up and go to the street called Straight, and inquire at the house of Judas for a man from Tarsus named Saul, for he is praying, **12** and he has seen in a vision a man named Ananias come in and lay his hands on him, so that he might regain his sight.

2. What does the Lord ask Ananias to do?

3. Read Acts 9:13-14. Then answer the questions that follow.

> **13** But Ananias answered, "Lord, I have heard from many about this man, how much harm he did to Your saints at Jerusalem; **14** and here he has authority from the chief priests to bind all who call on Your name."

    a. What did Ananias say back to the Lord? Write it out in your own words.

    b. Do you think he was afraid? Why would he be?

4. Now for the neatest part of the story! Read Acts 9:15-16.

> **15** But the Lord said to him, "Go, for he is a chosen instrument of Mine, to bear My name before the Gentiles and kings and the sons of Israel; **16** for I will show him how much he must suffer for My name's sake."

5. What does Jesus say about Saul?

    Isn't it neat to see that Jesus chose Saul even though Saul hated Jesus and those who followed Jesus?

6. Let's see what happened when Ananias went to pray for Saul. Again I'll help you out a little just because I do not want you to miss anything that happens! We'll find the end to our story in Acts 9:17-19.

> **17** So Ananias departed and entered the house, and after laying his hands on him said, "Brother Saul, the Lord Jesus, who appeared to you on the road by which you were coming, has sent me so that you may regain your sight and be filled with the Holy Spirit." **18** And immediately there fell from his eyes something like scales, and he regained his sight, and he got up and was baptized; **19** and he took food and was strengthened. Now for several days he was with the disciples who were at Damascus.

7. Ananias told Saul that the Lord Jesus sent him there so that two things may happen. Write below what Ananias said. I'll get you started.

    a. so that you may regain _____ _____ ,

    b. and be _____ _____ _____ _____ _____ .

8. What happened? Look back at Acts 9:18-19 in number 6 and fill in the answers.

a. And immediately there _____ _____ his eyes

something _____ _____ ,

b. and he _____ his sight,

c. and he got up and was _____ ,

d. and he took _____ and was _____ .

9. Read Acts 9:20 to see what Saul did after he regained his strength!

And immediately he *began* to proclaim Jesus in the synagogues, saying, "He is the Son of God."

When the Lord saves you, you want to tell others so that they can know Him too. That's what we see Saul begin to do.

10. Let's look at one last verse and discover the source of Paul's strength and boldness.

But, Saul, who was also *known as* Paul, filled with the Holy Spirit,…

11. Paul was filled with Someone who gave him a new life. Who was it?

Well, you've learned a lot about the man named Saul who became Paul.
Why don't you thank God today that He loves us even when we don't do things that
are very lovable. Thank Him that His kind of love never stops and that
He gives us a new life through His Spirit.

LAYER FIVE: A Man with a Mission

There are times when the Lord brings two people together so that they can do a job for Him. He knows that together they can do the job better than they could if they were trying to do it alone.

God brought Paul and Timothy together so that they could tell others about Him. Today we'll see how they met. We'll also see how Paul felt about Timothy.

1. We're going back to the book of Acts again. Let's examine Acts 15:36–16:4. It is a bit long, but I think you'll like reading it because you'll see how Paul prepares for a long journey. He is going back to many places he has been before to see how his friends are doing. He is trying to decide who should go with him. Read and see what happens.

36 After some days Paul said to Barnabas, "Let us return and visit the brethren in every city in which we proclaimed the word of the Lord, *and see* how they are." **37** Barnabas wanted to take John, called Mark, along with them also. **38** But Paul kept insisting that they should not take him along who had deserted them in Pamphylia and had not gone with them to the work. **39** And there occurred such a sharp disagreement that they separated from one another, and Barnabas took Mark with him and sailed away to Cyprus. **40** But Paul chose Silas and left, being committed by the brethren to the grace of the Lord. **41** And he was traveling through Syria and Cilicia, strengthening the churches.

Chapter 16

1 Paul came also to Derbe and to Lystra. And a disciple was there, named Timothy, the son of a Jewish woman who was a believer, but his father was a Greek, **2** and he was well spoken of by the brethren who were in Lystra and Iconium. **3** Paul wanted this man to go with him; and he took him and circumcised him because of the Jews who were in those parts, for they all knew that his father was a Greek. **4** Now while they were passing through the cities, they were delivering the decrees which had been decided upon by the apostles and elders who were in Jerusalem, for them to observe.

2. Let's look closer at what we read about Timothy. Look back at Acts 16:1-2 and let's note what we see about him.

    a. What was he called in verse 1?

    b. Do you know what a disciple is?

I think one easy way to define "disciple" is to say that a disciple is a follower of Jesus. It is someone who loves the Lord Jesus and wants to do all He asks them to do. Do you remember another name used for these people? That's right—the Way.

    c. What did you learn about Timothy's mother?

    d. What did you see about his father?

    e. What did other people think of Timothy? Look at verse 2 again.

We see that Paul took Timothy with him on his journey. This was the second trip that Paul was taking in order to tell people about Jesus and to see how the people he loved were doing.

We usually call these trips Paul's "Missionary Journeys." This trip he was taking with Timothy was Paul's "Second Missionary Journey."

3. Let's take a few more minutes and see what Paul says about Timothy when he writes to the Philippians. Read Philippians 2:20-22.

> **20** …I have no one *else* of kindred spirit who will genuinely be concerned for your welfare. **21** For they all seek after their own interests, not those of Christ Jesus. **22** But you know of his proven worth, that he served with me in the furtherance of the gospel like a child *serving* his father.

4. You see we have skipped over into chapter two of Philippians to do a little digging. You just read about a time after their journey together when Paul wanted to send Timothy back to check on the people there.

Let's do a new and fun exercise to see what you can learn about Timothy. You're going to make a list about Timothy!

List below what Paul says about Timothy in these verses. I'll help you out by titling the list and numbering it for you.

Clue #5: Some of what Paul tells them about Timothy is sort of hidden. You'll have to look at what he says that isn't true of others to get what he is trying to say about Timothy.

TIMOTHY

1.

2.

3.

4.

5. Try your hand at the Key Word Puzzle on page 30 to see what Timothy was.

We are almost finished for the week, but first let me ask you a question: You saw the good things that people said about Timothy; can people say good things about you?

If you're living in a way that would please the Lord, they can. Are you living that way? If you don't think you are, talk to your mom or dad and ask them to help you pray about this.

Thanks for hanging in there for this week. You have done a tremendous job to come to this point!

Next week we'll discover where this journey takes Paul and Timothy, and we'll also see what happens on the journey. See you then!

P.S.: Don't forget to record your Truth Treasures below! And Bury the Treasure! This week's verse is from the book of Romans. It says you are to renew your mind and that you are not to be conformed to the world. If you are conformed to the world, you think and act and talk like the world. BUT if you spend time studying the Word of God, you renew your mind and think like God wants you to think!

TRUTH TREASURES FOR THE WEEK

1.

2.

3.

BURY THE TREASURE:

And do not be conformed to this world, but be transformed by the renewing of your mind… (Romans 12:2a).

Paul and the Philippians

Questions about the author

- Who was with Timothy in Philippians 1:1? It begins with the letter "P."

- In verse 1, what do the men who wrote call themselves? It begins with a "B."

- Where were they when they wrote? Read Philippians 1:7. (You'll have to think really hard because Paul does not say exactly where he is, but he does give you a clue.)

- Look at Philippians 1:8 to see how Paul felt about the people he was writing to. What did you find out about them?

Questions about the people

- What are these people called in Philippians 1:1? "To all the _____ ."

- Where did they live? Read Philippians 1:1 again and give the name of the city.

- Now can you see why this book is called "Philippians?" Why?

Key Word Puzzle

To find the key word, fill in the blanks in words 1 though 8 with the correct missing letter.
Then transfer the letter from number 1 to number 1 below and so on through number 8.
When you have transferred all 8 letters, you'll have the key word.

1 L __ G H T   **5** T A R __ U S

2 __ A M A S C U S   **6** I S R A __ L

3 S A U __   **7** B A __ T I Z E D

4 V __ S I O N   **8** __ H U R C H

Key Word:

2	1	5	8	4	7	3	6

Dig 3

The Ancient City

Tools of the Trade

1. Colored pencils
2. Pen or pencil
3. Map on page 45
4. Chart: The Purpose of Paul's Letter to the Philippians on pages 42-43
5. Treasure Map on the book of Philippians on pages 155-160
6. Word Dig Crossword Puzzle on page 44

Directions for Diggers

Do you have mountains and rivers where you live? Or is your hometown near the ocean? Do you live near a city or a very large town?

Does it get really hot in the summer? Do you have thunderstorms in the summer and snow in the winter where you live? Does it rain often, or is it a dry climate?

If people live in a certain city, they do certain things. People who live near the mountains often hike or snow ski. They may fish in the rivers. Others who live near the ocean may wind surf or go crabbing. People who live in large cities may enjoy going to concerts, museums, or the zoo.

To understand people, it helps to understand the city they live in. When an archeologist wants to know about people who lived thousands of years ago, he will dig into the earth over the area where they lived looking for clues as to how they lived.

As he works, he puts all of the large pieces of pottery, all of the large stones, all of the big shards of glass in one area. He also keeps all of the dirt and puts it in very colorful buckets. When he is finished digging for the day, he will take all of the buckets and sift through the dirt to be sure he doesn't miss small treasures. He uses a sieve to do this. He will often have another person working on his team help with the sieve. He carefully considers all of the small items left in the sieve and decides what to keep and examine later.

Today, we'll begin to gather facts about Philippi, the colony where the Philippians lived. We'll sift through and even look for small treasure that will help our understanding. Through our observations, we'll begin to learn about these people who were so special to Paul.

Ready to dig in and sift through? Great! Let's do it!

LAYER ONE: Paul's Biggest Desire

1. Today we want to "chart the course" by tracing Paul's "Second Missionary Journey" on the map on page 45. You'll be able to see where Paul and Timothy traveled together on this long journey. Remember they traveled by ship.

Be sure to pay attention to each location you're marking so that you can see when they get to Philippi. Remember that the book we are studying was written to the people who live in Philippi—the Philippians!

At the bottom of the map, you'll see a list of the places Paul and Timothy visited on this journey. Use a dark colored pencil to mark each location on the map with a number. Mark the first spot number 1, the second number 2, and so on until you have marked all sixteen places on the map.

2. Now that you have located the places Paul and Timothy visited, draw a line to connect them. Begin with number 1 and draw your line to number 2 and so on until you reach number sixteen. When you finish, you'll have discovered the amazing journey that Paul and Timothy took!

3. As the two men made this very long journey, they shared the gospel— the good news of Jesus Christ. This was what Paul believed God had asked him to do.

Isn't it exciting to think that God has a work that He wants you to do? In the same way that He asked Paul and Timothy to travel and tell people about the gospel of Jesus Christ, He has something that He will ask you to do one day too.

You may be a teacher, a professional athlete, a photographer, a secretary, a housewife and mother, a janitor, a salesman, a butcher, a newspaper reporter, or an archaeologist. Whatever you do in life, God can use you to tell others about Him.

As a matter of fact, He can use you to share your truth treasures about Him with other boys and girls right now! And as you dig out more truth from His Word and as you discover more of how He works in the lives of people, you'll want to tell others about Him because He is so GREAT!

**You've done a good day's worth of digging.
Take a break and enjoy something that is especially
fun for you, and I'll see you tomorrow!**

LAYER TWO: Paul Takes a Stand in Philippi

I hope you have enjoyed digging out truth about Paul last week. And I'm sure you really liked seeing how he met Timothy! Isn't it neat to see how God gave them a special relationship and to see how they worked together?

Now let's see what we can uncover about the people they wrote this letter to—the Philippians, the people of Philippi. You discovered a few facts about them on our second dig. Now you'll dig out more truths to add to those!

You may wonder what all of this has to do with the book of Philippians, but hang in there and you'll see. It's important for you to know about this city and its people because then you'll understand what Paul wrote to them.

Let's get started! Don't forget to check in with headquarters as you begin today.

1. We're going back to the book of Acts to dig around and see what we can find about the city of Philippi and about its people. Remember that Acts tells us the story of Paul. Read Acts 16:11-12 and then write out two things you discover about the city of Philippi. I'll help you!

> **11** So putting out to sea from Troas, we ran a straight course to Samothrace, and on the day following Neapolis; **12** and from there to Philippi, which is a leading city of the district of Macedonia, a *Roman* colony; and we were staying in this city for some days.

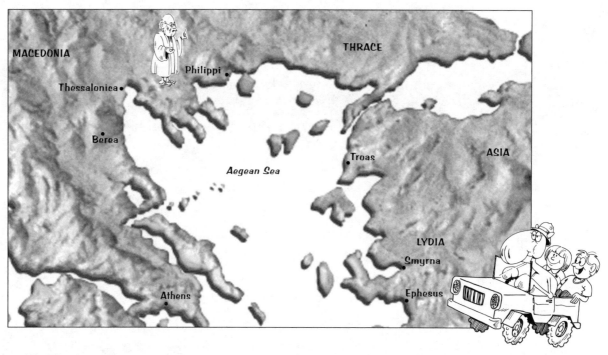

a. Philippi is a _____ _____ of the district of _____ ,

b. a _____ colony.

2. In Acts 20:6 the city of Philippi is mentioned again. You won't see anything in that verse that will really help with our study, but you can get a neat fact about the city if you think hard. It's sort of a "brain bender," so if you can't get it don't get stuck here. This treasure is at the very bottom layer! **Clue #6:** What is said in the verse that will tell you something about the location of the city. See if you can get it and write it below.

> We sailed from Philippi after the days of Unleavened Bread, and came to them at Troas within five days; and there we stayed seven days.

Philippi is a _____ _____ .

If you didn't figure it out, don't let it bother you. It is really a hidden treasure, but I thought you might like to try it. What we were looking for is that Philippi was a port city on the coast near the water. You can know that because you see that Paul sailed from there! Go back to the map above and locate the city again. Seeing it on the map will help you remember where it is!

3. Let's take a few minutes today to examine a couple of things about the people who lived in Philippi. Read 1 Thessalonians 2:1-2. What does Paul say happened to him in Philippi?

> **1** For you yourselves know, brethren, that our coming to you was not in vain,
> **2** but after we had already suffered and been mistreated in Philippi, as you
> know, we had the boldness in our God to speak to you the gospel of God
> amid much opposition.

So we know from these verses that there were some people in Philippi who did not like Paul and what he stood for.

4. Now look at Philippians 4:15-16 and see what Paul says some of the Philippians did for him.

> **15** You yourselves also know, Philippians, that at the first preaching of the gospel, after I left Macedonia, no church shared with me in the matter of giving and receiving but you alone; **16** for even in Thessalonica you sent *a gift* more than once for my needs.

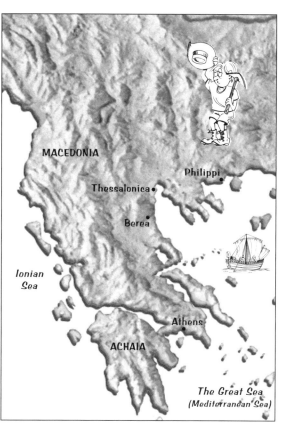

From these verses we find that there were also those in Philippi who loved and appreciated Paul.

It's interesting to realize that even a man like Paul had people who didn't think he was so great. It wasn't because Paul was being unkind or difficult. They didn't like him because he stood for something that they didn't like—the gospel.

The next time you think someone doesn't like you very much, think of Paul. But be sure that you aren't doing things to other people that would make them dislike you.

I hope you're enjoying discovering treasures about the people Paul loved so much. You're doing well. I know you're digging hard and deep. Hang in there with me because it'll get better and better.

Take a break. I am. See you soon!

LAYER THREE: An Attack Comes

Today let's dig together to see some of the events that happened while Paul was in Philippi. Again we'll be uncovering treasures in the book of Acts.

1. Read Acts 16:13-15 and write down what happened to a woman named Lydia.

> **13** And on the Sabbath day we went outside the gate to a riverside, where we were supposing that there would be a place of prayer; and we sat down and began speaking to the women who had assembled. **14** A woman named Lydia, from the city of Thyatira, a seller of purple fabrics, a worshiper of God, was listening; and the Lord opened her heart to respond to the things spoken

by Paul. **15** And when she and her household had been baptized, she urged us, saying, "If you have judged me to be faithful to the Lord, come into my house and stay." And she prevailed upon us.

2. Let's keep reading in Acts 16. This time begin in verse 16 and read through verse 18 to see what happened next. You'll read about a slave girl who had an evil spirit.

The spirit was called *a spirit of divination*. That means that it was an evil spirit from the devil that helped the girl tell people about the future. Let's see what happened when Paul addressed the evil spirit that was using the girl to speak.

16 It happened that as we were going to the place of prayer, a slave-girl having a spirit of divination met us, who was bringing her masters much profit by fortune-telling. **17** Following after Paul and us, she kept crying out, saying, "These men are bond-servants of the Most High God, who are proclaiming to you the way of salvation." **18** She continued doing this for many days. But Paul was greatly annoyed, and turned and said to the spirit, "I command you in the name of Jesus Christ to come out of her!" And it came out at that very moment.

a. First write down what the girl was doing that was making a lot of money for her master.

b. You see that she followed Paul and his friends for days shouting about them. What was she saying?

c. Were the girl's word true?

d. What finally happened when Paul became greatly annoyed by the spirit in this girl? **Clue #7:** "Annoyed" means that he was tired of what she was doing!

e. What happened when Paul spoke to the spirit?

You can get some very valuable treasures from what we see in this account. These are precious stones you can add to your treasure chest.

Stone 1—We can ⸺⸺⸺ evil spirit will speak what is true. In this case, although what the ⸺⸺⸺⸺⸺ ⸺⸺ being loud and going on and on. It was bothering pe⸺⸺⸺

The fact tha⸺⸺⸺⸺⸺⸺⸺⸺⸺⸺⸺⸺⸺ ⸺ing your sister or brother run around i⸺⸺⸺⸺⸺⸺⸺⸺⸺⸺⸺⸺ ⸺g to read your favorite book. It makes it ⸺⸺⸺⸺⸺⸺⸺⸺⸺⸺s shouting made it hard to take care of th⸺⸺

St⸺ ⸺⸺⸺⸺⸺⸺⸺⸺⸺⸺ when he spoke to it. You'll see that Paul ⸺⸺⸺⸺⸺⸺⸺⸺⸺⸺u can always know that Jesus is st⸺⸺⸺⸺⸺⸺⸺⸺⸺⸺rraid of what the enemy can do. You

⸺⸺⸺⸺⸺⸺⸺⸺t else happened to Paul while he was in ⸺⸺⸺⸺⸺u're uncovering.

⸺⸺⸺⸺ all of the truth treasures you are gathering ⸺⸺⸺ays that will always please Him.

⸺OUR: Paul Goes to Prison

Let's dig some mo⸺⸺⸺ ⸺6 and see what else we can find about Paul's time in Philippi. There are lots of q⸺⸺ions, but lots of great action too! What a story!

1. Remember, we ended yesterday with the story about the slave girl. She was being used by some men to make money. She had an evil spirit that helped her tell people's fortunes. Paul commanded the spirit to leave, and it did.

Read Acts 16:19-21 to see how the men who had used the slave girl to make money reacted to what Paul did. Write what you learn below.

> **19** But when her masters saw that their hope of profit was gone, they seized Paul and Silas and dragged them into the market place before the authorities, **20** and when they had brought them to the chief magistrates, they said, "These men are throwing our city into confusion, being Jews, **21** and are proclaiming customs which it is not lawful for us to accept or to observe, being Romans."

2. Now let's take a look at Acts 16:22-24 to see what happened to Paul and Silas as a result of the men being so angry.

> **22** The crowd rose up together against them, and the chief magistrates tore their robes off them and proceeded to order *them* to be beaten with rods.

23 When they had struck them with many blows, they threw them into prison, commanding the jailer to guard them securely; **24** and he, having received such a command, threw them into the inner prison and fastened their feet in stocks.

3. If you'll record the treasures you find by answering the following questions, you'll have a record of what happened.

    a. What did the crowd do?

    b. What did the chief magistrates do?

    c. After they beat the men, what did they do with them?

    d. What did they tell the jailer?

    e. What did the jailer do?

4. Now read Acts 16:25-34. Don't get tired of digging. There's lots more to unearth.

25 But about midnight Paul and Silas were praying and singing hymns of praise to God, and the prisoners were listening to them; **26** and suddenly there came a great earthquake, so that the foundations of the prison house were shaken; and immediately all the doors were opened and everyone's chains were unfastened. **27** When the jailer awoke and saw the prison doors opened, he drew his sword and was about to kill himself, supposing that the prisoners had escaped. **28** But Paul cried out with a loud voice, saying, "Do not harm yourself, for we are all here!" **29** And he called for lights and rushed in, and trembling with fear he fell down before Paul and Silas, **30** and after he brought them out, he said, "Sirs, what must I do to be saved?" **31** They said, "Believe in the Lord Jesus, and you will be saved, you and your household." **32** And they spoke the word of the Lord to him together with all who were in his house. **33** And he took them that *very* hour of the night and washed their wounds, and immediately he was baptized, he and all of his *household*.

34 And he brought them into his house and set food before them, and rejoiced greatly, having believed in God with his whole household.

5. Again, answer the questions so that you have all that happened in writing.
   a. What were Paul and Silas doing?

   b. What happened next? (Read verse 26.)

   c. What did the guard start to do? Why?

   d. What did Paul do?

   e. What did the guard ask Paul and Silas?

   f. What answer did Paul and Silas give him?

   g. Who did they also tell this truth to?

   h. What did the guard do for them?

   i. Did the guard believe on Jesus? Did his family?

After all of this happened, Paul left Philippi and traveled to Thessalonica to be with other people who needed to know about Jesus. Paul knew that many people needed to know about Jesus and what He had done to set them free from sin.

As you play with your friends…
As you go to the grocery store with your mom…
As you go to the pool in the summer or the library in the winter…
As you go to the video store with your dad…
(Remember people need to know about Jesus.)

**As you practice what you learn, people will know that you're different.
Just by the way you live, you'll be telling people about Jesus!**

LAYER FIVE: Paul Loved the People

We have dug out treasures about Paul, Timothy, the city of Philippi, and the people who live there. We have seen how much Paul loves these people too. So now let's dig for some of the reasons he wrote this important letter.

1. Today let's "chart the course" so we can discover why Paul wrote this letter to the people in Philippi. The chart is called The Purpose of Paul's Letter to the Philippians and is on pages 42-43.

This course will be easy to chart. Just read the verses I have listed for you in the left-hand column. Then in the space in the right-hand column, write down what you dig out from these verses about why Paul wrote this letter. Remember to use your "Treasure Map" in the back of your book.

You'll discover many different things Paul shared with these people he loved! When you read the book of Philippians on your own, you may see some reasons that are not listed here. We're not going to look at all of the reasons. We'll look at just some of the main ones. Go ahead and fill in the chart, then come back to number 2.

2. Why do *you* think Paul wrote this letter to the Philippians? Try to write just a sentence or two that explains what you think now that you have dug through these verses. You may have more than one reason!

3. I'm sure you saw how much Paul loved the people at Philippi and how much he wanted them to do well and be used by God. There were no telephones or e-mail, so letters were the best way to communicate when people were in two different locations.

Think of someone you love who you want to know how you feel—maybe a grandparent or a friend who lives in another city. Why don't you write them a note over the weekend telling them you're thinking about them and that you're digging through the letter Paul wrote to the people he loved in Philippi. I know they will be encouraged to hear from you.

I am proud of you for digging through all five layers of this week's dig, and I pray that you realize how much you're learning and how much the treasures you're gathering will help you become a young man or young woman who God can use—wherever you are! Remember to record this week's Truth Treasures below.

This week the treasure you'll bury in your heart is out of the book of Philippians. As Paul opens his letter to these people he loves, he tells them that he is confident of one thing—that God will finish the work He is doing in them. He uses the words *perfect it* to mean *finish it*.

As you study this letter Paul wrote, you'll see that he talks with them about things that he thinks will help them along the way as God does this work in them.

You can be encouraged today by this verse too because it is true for you—just like it was for the Philippians!

For those of you who want the ultimate Philippians challenge, try the Word Dig Crossword Puzzle on page 44.

**Have a good break. Do something fun.
I'll catch up with you for Dig Four in a day or so!**

TRUTH TREASURES FOR THE WEEK

1.

2.

3.

BURY THE TREASURE:

For I am confident of this very thing, that He who began a good work in you will perfect it until the day of Christ Jesus (Philippians 1:6).

The Purpose of Paul's Letter to the Philippians

Verses to Read	Why Paul Wrote the Letter
Philippians 1:12 (Note that the circumstances he mentions is the fact that he is in prison.)	
Philippians 1:27	
Philippians 2:2	
Philippians 2:3	
Philippians 2:14	
Philippians 2:16	

Philippians 3:2

Philippians 3:17

Philippians 4:1

Philippians 4:4

Philippians 4:5

Philippians 4:8

Word Dig Crossword Puzzle

Look at the definition for each word you are trying to dig out. There is also a clue about which layer to dig back through to find the word. As you unearth your find, write the word in its numbered space.

This puzzle is a real challenge. You'll have to dig and dig to finish it, but you'll have great fun! Go for it!

Across

5. Another word for guard (Layer 4)
6. Time of night when Paul was pray-ing and singing (Layer 4)
7. A port city near Philippi (Layer 2)
9. A Roman colony (Layer 2)
11. What did the jailer do (Layer 4)
12. What Paul preached (Layer 2)
13. Lydia & household were (Layer 3)

Down

1. The city nearby Philippi (Layer 3)
2. What Lydia sold (Layer 3)
3. What shook the prison (Layer 4)
4. Where they sent Paul (Layer 4)
8. Leading city of the district (Layer 2)
10. What the jailer did after they reached his home (Layer 4)
12. Sent more than once (Layer 2)

PAUL AND TIMOTHY'S JOURNEY

(ON THE ABOVE MAP, PLACE THE PROPER NUMBER BY EACH CITY.)

1. Phrygia
2. Galatia
3. Mysia
4. Troas
5. Samothrace
6. Neapolis
7. Philippi
8. Amphipolis
9. Apollonia
10. Thessalonica
11. Berea
12. Athens
13. Corinth
14. Syria
15. Ephesus
16. Caesarea

Dig 4

Seekers in Sneakers—
Alias "Jr. Saints"

Tools of the Trade

1. Pen
2. Colored Pencils
3. Bible
4. Seeking Saints Word Search on page 56

Directions for Diggers

Don't forget that the most important thing you can do when you begin your dig each week is to check in with headquarters. Ask the Holy Spirit to help you understand what you discover in God's Word. Have you checked in as you begin? If not, stop now and pray.

This dig is an important one, so be sure to give yourself enough time to get to the bottom of each layer. I think you'll be excited to uncover truth about this week's topic because I know you'll want to become the kind of person that you'll find out about as you dig.

Ready? Let's get digging!

LAYER ONE: Serving Christ Is Freedom

Do you remember that in Dig Two we charted some facts about Paul (the author of the book of Philippians) and about the Philippians (the people the book of Philippians was written to)? When the chart was complete, we had unearthed the facts that Paul and Timothy were called "bond-servants" and that the Philippians were called "saints."

1. Today we want to take out our sieve and carefully sift through the Word to understand what it means to be a bond-servant. First, record below what you think a servant is.

2. In Old Testament times, if you were sold into slavery, you had to serve your master for a very long time. Do you know how long? **Clue #8:** Deuteronomy 15 gives us some clues about people who decided to become bond-servants. If a person was sold into slavery, he had to serve his master for six years. But the law made the master set him free in the seventh year. When the master set the slave free, he also had to give the slave food and supplies to get him started in a new life.

Examine Deuteronomy 15:16-17. You'll observe that sometimes when a slave was to be set free, he wanted to stay with his master.

> **16** "It shall come about if he says to you, 'I will not go out from you,' because he loves you and your household, since he fares well with you; **17** then you shall take an awl and pierce it through his ear into the door, and he shall be your servant forever. Also you shall do likewise to your maidservant."

3. Dig into verse 16 to find three reasons why someone would want to become a bond-servant. Let's do another Lipogram to find these reasons.

Because he l _ _ e s _ o u

Because he _ _ _ e s y _ _ r h _ _ _ _ h _ _ _

Because he f _ _ _ _ w _ _ _ _ _ _ h _ _ u

> (This means that the master has taken good care of the slave and that the slave has been happy with the master's family.)

4. Observe verse 17 more closely and note how long someone had to serve as a bond-servant if they decided to become one.

5. You found in verse 17 that the master was to take an awl and pierce the ear of the person who decided to become a bond-servant.

A Special Find: An awl is a tool that it used to put a small hole in leather. It was also used to put a small hole in the ear of the bond-servant so that the bond-servant could wear a distinctive earring that would show others that he belonged to his master.

The ear of the bond-servant was placed against the facing of a door which was used as a brace so that the hole could be placed in the ear. It may sound horrible, but it would be sort of like someone getting their ear pierced today—not so bad!

6. Now dig into Galatians 1:10 and find what Paul calls himself in that verse. Record it below.

7. Why do you think someone would decide to become the bond-servant of Jesus Christ? Go back to number 3 and review the reasons a slave would become a bond-servant to their master.

8. What has Christ done for mankind that should make each one of us want to serve as His bond-servant? Read Romans 5:6-8 and write these verses out below.

This time, you do the writing, because I know it'll help you to remember finding this treasure—more so than if I do it for you.

9. Read out loud the treasure you've just found. What were we when Christ died for us? (Dig in verse 8.)

10. When you take Romans 5:6 in your hand and turn it over and over to examine it, what treasure do you find about us? What does it mean to be helpless?

11. Why do you think we are helpless when we are lost without Christ?

Isn't it because there is nothing we can do to save ourselves?

12. How did Christ help us? What did He do for us?

13. Are you a bond-servant of Jesus Christ? Do you think you should be? Why, or why not?

Thank the Lord Jesus Christ today for being willing to die for you so that you could be free to decide whom you want to serve.

As you complete your dig for today, ask God to help you understand what it really means to be His bond-servant.

LAYER TWO: Set Apart for God

Yesterday we dug around to see what it meant to be a bond-servant. Today we'll unearth another term Paul uses in his letter to the Philippians. It is something he calls them. The word is *saint*.

Let's spend some time discovering what it means to be a saint. Don't forget to ask the Holy Spirit to help you see and understand truth.

A Special Find: A saint is a person who knows the Lord Jesus Christ. He or she has been saved and now follows Jesus. A saint's life belongs to Christ, and he wants to please Jesus in all that he does. Saints are set apart. That means they don't live like the people in the world around them who don't know Jesus Christ. Those people are living to please themselves or others. In the Word of God, saints are sometimes called "holy."

Let's observe a couple of scriptures and see what we can uncover about those who are holy or set apart for God's purposes.

1. Read 2 Corinthians 6:14.

> Do not be bound together with unbelievers; for what partnership have righteousness and lawlessness, or what fellowship has light with darkness?

a. According to this verse, what kind of relationship are you to have with those who don't believe in Jesus?

You see you are not to be bound together with an unbeliever. An unbeliever is someone who isn't a bond-servant of Jesus.

Do you know what it means to be bound to an unbeliever? I think we can say that it means you're in a relationship with that person.

Then we see the verse talk about light and dark. What are those two words? They are opposites. So the verse is saying that someone who loves God and someone who doesn't love God should not be bound together.

You may wonder why. I think being bound to someone who doesn't love God could make it harder for you to be what Christ wants you to be. It would be a relationship that could take your time and attention away from what Jesus wants for you.

2. Dig through John 17:15. This verse is a part of a prayer that Jesus prayed for all those who would believe in Him and ask Him to be their Savior and Lord.

> "I do not ask You to take them out of the world, but to keep them from the evil *one*."

3. Did you discover that Jesus doesn't want you to be taken out of the world? He knows you have to be around people who don't love Him and obey Him because the world is full of people like that. But remember what you saw in 2 Corinthians 6:14.

Remember not to spend too much time with people who will take you away from what Jesus wants for you. If you love Him and want to obey Him, He has set you apart for His plans. You don't want to do anything that would keep you from being able to do all that He wants you to do!

Even at your age, it is important to decide if you want to be set apart for what God wants to do in your life. Today tell Him that you want to understand what it means to be set apart. We'll talk more about all of this tomorrow.

But for today, how about a fun game? Turn to page 56 and do the puzzle called "Seeking Saints."

Great digging! You mined some amazing truths today. Treasure them!

LAYER THREE: Who Do You Belong To?

Remember that we are looking at what it means to be a saint, to be set apart for God's purposes. AND we are trying to understand what it means to be His bond-servant.

1. If you want to be set apart for what God wants to do in your life, you must come to Him and tell Him that you'll live for Him and do what *He* wants you to do—not what *you* want to do.

Being a bond-servant means that you have a master. You don't make decisions or choices without asking Him what He wants you to do. Then when He tells you what it is, you're obedient.

2. Maybe you think that you'd like to be in charge of your own life rather than having a master. Well, let's look at a verse that will help you see why you really don't have that choice. Read Acts 26:18.

> to open their eyes so that they may turn from darkness to light and from the
> dominion of Satan to God, in order that they may receive forgiveness of sins
> and an inheritance among those who have been sanctified by faith in Me.

Think hard about what you just read. You can see that you may turn from _____ to _____ or from the dominion (or power) of _____ to _____.

3. From what you observe in the verse above, if you don't belong to God, who has control of your life?

4. Does it surprise you that the Bible is so clear? Let's look at one more example of what God says about someone who doesn't yet belong to Him. Read Romans 5:10 and circle the word that describes this person who is not yet reconciled to God, who isn't God's friend yet.

> For if while we were enemies, we were reconciled to God through the death of
> His Son, much more, having been reconciled, we shall be saved by His life.

5. If you don't side with Jesus Christ and do what He wants you to do, you're living in darkness and are an enemy of God. You may not have known this, and you may not want to be on the side of darkness—but if you aren't a Christian, that is the truth.

Tell Jesus today what you want to do and who you want to serve. But just remember how long a bond-servant is to serve. It is the same when you become a bond-servant of the Lord Jesus. How long is it? Write below if you want to be a bond-servant of Jesus and explain why or why not.

See you when you tackle Layer Four.

LAYER FOUR: How Satan Gained Control

Today we'll talk about how Satan gained control, about why you have to decide who you will serve, who you will follow. It would be a good idea to ask your mom or dad to go on this dig with you. It may be a little hard to understand some of the truths we'll dig out today, but it's important to try. If one of your parents can't work with you, then be sure to tag anything you dig out that you don't understand so you can talk with them or your teacher later. (Remember when an archaeologist digs all day that at the end of the day's work he *tags* his finds. He uses the tag to identify where he found his treasure and to note anything special about it.)

Ask God to help you understand truth. Pray that you'll see whose team you're on now.

1. In Genesis 3 the serpent tempted Eve and Adam, and they listened to the serpent and did what he said instead of believing God.

In that moment when the devil deceived Eve and she and Adam ate the fruit, Satan gained control over all mankind. And man was separated from God.

2. Sin separated man from God. The Bible says in Romans 5:19, that "…through the one man's disobedience, the many were made sinners,…"
Who was this one man?

3. When Adam disobeyed god, it affected all mankind. What does the Bible say is the penalty or wage for sin? Read Romans 6:23a below for the answer.

For the wages of sin is death…

4. Read 1 Corinthians 15:21-22 below and circle the word that tells you how many died because of Adam's sin.

21 For since by a man *came* death, by a man also *came* the resurrection of the dead. **22** For as in Adam all die, so also in Christ all will be made alive.

This all sounds like pretty bad news, doesn't it? But Jesus came to bring good news! He came to give you life! He came so that you would have a choice about whose team you'd be on. He made a way for you to be a saint, a bond-servant. Tomorrow we'll see how.

**You've done a lot of hard work.
So take a break and grab a snack.**

LAYER FIVE: How Jesus Sets Us Free

Before you become a Christian, you can't always do what is right, even if you want to. Because of Adam's sin, you are a slave to sin! It is like you are in a room with the door locked and there is no way out. The devil has the key, and he wants you to stay right there in that room.

It doesn't matter how hard you try to get out, it is impossible. You may peek under the door and see a ray of light, but you can't get out! You may even try to climb up the wall so that you can sneak a peek out the window, but it doesn't matter if you can see out. You can't get out! You are locked in, and it seems there is no way out!

1. But the good news is that there is a way out. Let's read 1 John 3:8b.

    ...The Son of God appeared for this purpose, to destroy the works of the devil.

What did Jesus come to do?

2. Did you discover a great truth? Did you find that when Jesus came He destroyed the devil's plan? That's great news, isn't it? Jesus came to set you free! Jesus came so you could be a saint instead of a sinner!

3. Remember that the wages of sin is death. But because Jesus died for you and conquered death, you can be free! You don't have to stay locked in the room. The devil doesn't have the key any longer. Jesus does!
Read Revelation 1:18 and see what Jesus says.

    ...I was dead, and behold, I am alive forevermore, and I
    have the keys of death and of Hades.

Who has the keys of death and of Hades?

4. Now, let's look back and remember what we read in Layer Four and add the rest of the story. Read 1 Corinthians 15:22.

    For as in Adam all die, so also in Christ all will be made alive.

Does part of this verse look familiar? We read in Layer Four that *in Adam* all died. Now we know the rest of the story. What happens to all who are *in Christ?*

5. Remember in Layer Four you also learned that the wages of sin is death. Now we know Jesus conquered death and made us alive in Him. Look up Romans 6:23 and write out the whole verse so that you never forget it.

6. Circle above in the verse you wrote what the Bible tells you is God's free gift to those who are in Christ Jesus.

7. For the last time, think back to Layer Four where you read Romans 5:19 and saw what happened because of Adam's disobedience. Now reread Romans 5:19 on the next page and see what happened because of Christ's obedience.

> For as through the one man's disobedience the many were made sinners, even so through the obedience of the One the many will be made righteous.

What good news! Because of Jesus you can be righteous—a saint, a bond-servant of Jesus—a free man—a friend of God! Have you decided to be His bond-servant? Talk to your mom or dad about what you're thinking at this point and ask them to pray with you. Remember not only can you become a bond-servant of Christ, you'll also be a SAINT—someone set apart for God to use to tell others about Him!

You've done a fantastic job! This has been a tough dig, and you've made it. Take a break and enjoy something fun you like to do.

TRUTH TREASURES FOR THE WEEK

1.

2.

3.

BURY THE TREASURE:

For am I now seeking the favor of men, or of God? Or am I striving to please men? If I were still trying to please men, I would not be a bond-servant of Christ (Galatians 1:10).

SEEKING SAINTS

See how many times you can find the word "saints" and circle it. Be sure to look up and down and side to side. It is okay if your circles overlap. There are 25 hidden "saints" in the

```
S  A  I  N  T  S  A  I  N  T  S  A  S  T
I  T  S  A  I  N  T  S  N  T  A  N  A  S
S  S  I  S  A  I  N  T  S  T  I  S  I  A
S  A  I  N  T  S  T  T  A  N  N  A  N  I
S  I  S  N  A  N  S  S  I  T  T  I  T  N
S  N  A  T  N  S  A  I  N  T  S  N  S  T
A  T  I  S  S  A  I  N  T  S  A  T  S  S
I  S  N  S  S  I  N  N  S  A  I  S  T  A
N  A  T  S  T  N  T  A  N  T  N  A  S  T
T  I  S  S  T  T  S  S  S  T  T  I  A  N
S  N  N  N  S  S  A  I  N  T  S  N  I  T
S  T  S  A  I  N  T  S  T  S  A  T  N  S
S  S  A  I  N  T  S  A  I  N  T  S  T  S
T  T  S  S  T  T  S  S  S  A  A  T  S  T
```

Dig 5

"Calling Headquarters! Come in, God"

Tools of the Trade

1. Colored pencils
2. Pen or pencil
3. Treasure Map on the book of Philippians on pages 155-160
4. Word Search on page 68

Directions for Diggers

Isn't it exciting to dig into God's Word and see what you can discover all by yourself? When I spend time studying the Word, I feel like a treasure hunter who comes back from his journey with his pockets full of gold.

This week we are going to dig out more golden nuggets of truth from the book of Philippians.

LAYER ONE: Talk to Him

Prayer is simply talking to God. It's a lot like talking with your parents or someone who loves you very much. You might share with them all about the things that have happened during the day or how you are happy or sad or need something. You like to share with them because they care very much about you and your needs.

That's the same reason you should talk to the heavenly Father in prayer. He cares very much about all that you do and are! For the next few days, we want to dig through five more layers and see what we can find in the Bible about prayer.

1. Read Philippians 1:1-11 aloud. Don't forget to use the "Treasure Map" on pages 155-160.

2. Read Philippians 1:1-11 again. Take the tool of your red pencil and circle the words *pray* or *prayer*. This will help you uncover all that is said about prayer when you finish.

3. Look back to what you've marked on prayer to help you with these questions.
   a. Who did Paul pray for?

   b. When did Paul pray for them?

   c. How did he pray for them? (Don't make this question hard. The simple answer is in verse 4.)

   d. Why did he pray for them? (Look in verse 5.)

   e. What did he pray for on their behalf? (You only need to dig in verse 9.)

Good job! You've started on a great dig today. One that will end in your knowing more about talking to the heavenly Father about things that matter most to you. See you next time!

LAYER TWO: Pray for Those You Love

The Bible tells us a lot about whom we are to pray for. Yesterday we saw that Paul prayed for the saints at Philippi because he loved them. He also prayed because he wanted them to know more and more about God so that they would be able to obey God.

Let's dig into some other places in the Bible that talk about praying for other Christians.

1. In Colossians chapter 1 Paul gives thanks to God for the saints at Colossae because they have faith in Christ Jesus and because they are obeying God. These people were his friends too. Read Colossians 1:9-12 and answer the questions that follow.

> **9** For this reason also, since the day we heard *of it*, we have not ceased to pray for you and to ask that you may be filled with the knowledge of His will in all spiritual wisdom and understanding, **10** so that you will walk in a manner worthy of the Lord, to please *Him* in all respects, bearing fruit in every good work and increasing in the knowledge of God; **11** strengthened with all power, according to His glorious might, for the attaining of all steadfastness and patience; joyously **12** giving thanks to the Father, who has qualified us to share in the inheritance of the saints in Light.

   a. How long did Paul pray for the Christians at Colossae?

   b. What did Paul ask for them? To see what he asks, look back at Colossians 1:9-12 as your guide and draw a line to connect the verbs with the nouns.

Filled with	**every good work.**
Walk in manner	**the knowledge of His will.**
Bearing fruit in	**all power.**
Increasing in	**thanks to the Father.**
Strengthened with	**worthy of the Lord.**
Attaining of all	**the knowledge of God.**
Joyously giving	**steadfastness and patience.**

2. In Colossians 4 another Christian, Epaphras, also prays for the saints at Colossae. Read Colossians 4:12.

> Epaphras, who is one of your number, a bondslave of Jesus Christ, sends you his greetings, always laboring earnestly for you in his prayers, that you may stand perfect and fully assured in all the will of God.

   a. When does Epaphras pray for the Christians?

b. What is his prayer for them? Fill in the blanks to see it.

that you may _____ _____ and _____ _____ in all

the will of God.

3. In Ephesians 1, we find Paul praying for Christians again. This time he is praying for the saints at Ephesus—more friends. Read Ephesians 1:15-19.

> **15** For this reason I too, having heard of the faith in the Lord Jesus which *exists* among you and your love for all the saints, **16** do not cease giving thanks for you, while making mention *of you* in my prayers; **17** that the God of our Lord Jesus Christ, the Father of glory, may give to you a spirit of wisdom and of revelation in the knowledge of Him. **18** *I pray that* the eyes of your heart may be enlightened, so that you will know what is the hope of His calling, what are the riches of the glory of His inheritance in the saints, **19** and what is the surpassing greatness of His power toward us who believe. *These are* in accordance with the working of the strength of His might.

a. How long did Paul pray for them?

b. Fill in the lipogram to see the gifts Paul asked for the saints:

Verse 17: s _ i r i t o f w _ _ _ _ m

   k n _ _ l e _ g _ o f H _ m

Verse 18: e _ e s o f y _ _ _ h e a r t m a y b e e n _ _ g h t _ _ e d

c. What does Paul want them to know?

Verse 18: h _ _ e o f H _ s c a _ _ i n g

   r i c h _ _ o f t h e g l _ _ y o f H _ s i n h _ _ i t _ _ c e

Verse 19: g r _ _ t _ _ s s o f H _ s p _ w e r

d. Paul knows God will answer his prayer for these Christians. You can see he knows this by completing the lipogram below.

Verse 19: these are in accordance with the
   _ _ _ _ i n g of the s t r _ _ _ t h o f H _ s m i _ _ t

This means that Paul prayed for things that he knew God would want to do for these people.

4. We have sifted through several verses that tell us how Paul prayed for the saints. Now let's look at Ephesians 6:18.

With all prayer and petition pray at all times in the Spirit, and with this in view, be on the alert with all perseverance and petition for all the saints.

a. Who does Paul tell them to pray for?

b. When are they to pray?

5. In Ephesians 6:19-20 Paul asks the Ephesians to pray for a specific saint.

19 and *pray* on my behalf, that utterance may be given to me in the opening of my mouth, to make known with boldness the mystery of the gospel, **20** for which I am an ambassador in chains; that in *proclaiming* it I may speak boldly, as I ought to speak.

a. Who does Paul want them to pray for?

b. Do the Word Search on page 68 to see what Paul wants them to pray for him.

c. Why do you think Paul needed to be bold?

Another great day of digging—on a very important topic. Great job! Put away your tools and take a well-deserved break. See you next time.

Layer Three: Stone Upon Stone

1. We've discovered the building stones of prayer. Let's review what you found about praying for other Christians.

Stone 1—According to Paul's example and instructions, we are to pray for other Christians.

Stone 2—We are to pray for them without ceasing. That means we don't stop praying. We pray regularly for these people.

Stone 3—We are to pray that…

- they will know God better
- they will know God's will
- they will obey God

Stone 4—We are to especially pray for the Christians that God has sent to help us know Him better. We should pray that…

- God will help them know exactly what to say to each person
- they will say it boldly (not holding back truth)

2. Now let's see how you can begin to practice some of the truths you've unearthed. Building a strong life of prayer with these stories of prayer takes time, but it's worth it! Let's get started.

Do you have some Christian friends who are having a hard time obeying what God says? Are some of your friends starting to listen to what the world says more than what God says? Do some of your friends have problems that are making them unhappy? These friends need you to pray for them.

List their names in the space below and spend some time praying for them right now. Then come back to the following list to see some ways you can pray for them…

- Pray that God will help them to know how much disobedience hurts Him.
- Pray that God will help you be an example to them.
- Pray that they will see how God can give them the strength and wisdom they need to face the problems in their lives.

FRIENDS TO PRAY FOR

3. Do you have Christian friends who want to know more and more about God? Do you have friends who love to read the Bible and pray? Do you have friends who want to do what pleases God more than what pleases the world?

They need your prayers also. List the names of these friends below and spend some time praying for them.

- Pray that their desire to please God will grow and grow.
- Pray that God will show you ways to encourage them.
- Pray that God will give you the courage to stand by them when someone makes fun of them.

FELLOW TREASURE HUNTERS TO PRAY FOR

4. Is there someone whom God is using to teach you and others about Himself? Do your parents teach you about God? What about the pastor of your church or your Sunday school or school teacher? Is there a neighbor or a good friend who helps you learn about the ways of God?

Write down the names of these people also.

- Pray that they will continue to know God more and more so that they can help other people know Him more.
- Pray that God would show them the right words to say to each person they try to help.
- Pray that they will not be afraid to teach people about God.

MASTER DIGGERS TO PRAY FOR

5. You've just started prayer lists. In Layer Two, we saw that we are to pray for Christians all the time, not just once. You can remember to pray for them by using a prayer list and putting it where you'll be sure to see it.

Decide where you want to put your prayer list. Then copy the names that you just listed in your workbook to a sheet of paper, a card, a notebook, or whatever will be the best for you. Then put it in that location so that you'll be reminded to pray again tomorrow.

You might want to put the list on the bulletin board in your room. Or maybe you would like to have it on a piece of paper that you can put in your Bible. If you keep a journal or diary, that would be a good place for your prayer list.

6. There is one other thing that I want you to do on your prayer list. Each time God answers a prayer that you've prayed for someone, write down how the prayer was answered and the date beside that person's name. It is very exciting to read back through your prayer list and see how God has answered your prayers.

LAYER FOUR: Learning to Pray

It was really neat to pray for your Christian friends, wasn't it?
Today we are going to look at someone else that God tells us to pray for.

1. Read Matthew 5:43-45.

> **43** "You have heard that it was said, 'You shall love your neighbor and hate your enemy.' **44** "But I say to you, love you enemies and pray for those who persecute you, **45** so that you may be sons of your Father who is in heaven; for He causes His sun to rise on *the* evil and *the* good, and sends rain on *the* righteous and *the* unrighteous.

a. Who are you told to pray for?

b. Fill in the blanks to review why you are to pray for them.

so that you may be _____ _____ _____ _____

who is in heaven; for He causes His sun to rise on the _____ and

the _____ , and sends rain on the _____ and the

_____ .

2. In Luke 6:27-28 God gives us more instructions about how to respond to our enemies. See if you can unearth those.

> **27** "But I say to you who hear, love your enemies, do good to those who hate you, **28** bless those who curse you, pray for those who mistreat you."

3. If you're really digging for God's truth, enemies will bother you or cause trouble. List four things you see in the verses above about how you are to respond to your enemies.

1.

2.

3.

4.

4. Luke 6:35 tells us why we are to respond to our enemies in this way. Write out why below.

"But love your enemies, and do good, and lend, expecting nothing in return; and your reward will be great, and you will be sons of the Most High; for He Himself is kind to ungrateful and evil *men*.

5. Let's add some names to the prayer list you made yesterday. I'm going to give you more time today because it is harder to pray for people who are being unkind to you.

Is there someone who makes fun of you and teases you about being a Christian? Is there someone who tries to push you into doing things that would not please God? Write those names in the space that follows and pray for them.

- Pray that God will show them how they are breaking His heart.
- Pray that God will help you respond in a kind, loving way when someone is making fun of you.
- Ask God to show you one act of kindness that you could do to show His love to that person.

People Who Are Unkind

5. Copy these names to your prayer list and continue to pray for them. Don't forget to record when a prayer is answered.

Layer Five: Trusting God

We have dug into prayer this week. We have prayed for our Christian friends, and we have prayed for our enemies. Today let's find some other instructions regarding prayer that God has given to us in His Word.

1. Read Philippians 4:6-7. ("Be anxious for nothing" means don't worry about anything.)

6 Be anxious for nothing, but in everything by prayer and supplication with thanksgiving let your requests be made known to God. 7 And the peace of God, which surpasses all comprehension will guard your hearts and your minds in Christ Jesus.

   a. What are you supposed to do instead of worrying?

   b. What will be the result be?

2. Read 1 Thessalonians 5:16-18

16 Rejoice always; 17 pray without ceasing; 18 in everything give thanks; for this is God's will for you in Christ Jesus.

   a. How often are we suppose to pray?

   b. What does that mean?

   c. How often are we supposed to rejoice?

   d. What are we suppose to give thanks for?

   e. Why?

3. Mark 11:25-26 tells us about something else that must be part of our prayers. Can you find it? It is just one word!

25 "Whenever you stand praying, forgive, if you have anything against any-one, so that your Father who is in heaven will also forgive you your transgressions. 26 "But is you do not forgive, neither will your Father who is in heaven forgive your transgressions."

   a. Why is it important that we forgive the things we are holding against someone?

b. Are you holding a grudge against someone? Are you angry at someone because he hurt your feelings? Ask God to show you if there is someone that you need to forgive. Write their name below.

Now ask God to help you forgive them, whether or not they ever apologize.

Your dig on the topic of prayer is over. Is it hard to believe? It is for me. I am happy that I had time to dig through all of these verses on prayer with you. I discovered some new truths about prayer as we studied.

I pray today that you'll keep on keeping on when it comes to praying for the people God has put in your life! And I pray that you'll want to learn more about prayer as you grow!

Now take what you've learned and pray! But first record your treasures.

TRUTH TREASURES FOR THE WEEK

1.

2.

3.

BURY THE TREASURE:

Be anxious for nothing, but in everything by prayer and supplication, with thanksgiving, let your requests be made known to God (Philippians 4:6).

WORD SEARCH

Paul wanted to preach the gospel, but he needed something so he asked his friends to pray. In four moves, discover what Paul needed to be when he preached the Word of God.

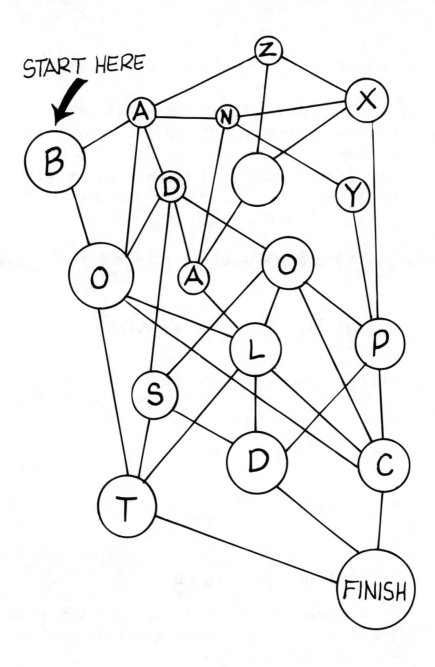

Dig 6

Be Strong! Be Bold!
The Lord Your God Is with You!

Tools of the Trade

1. Colored pencils
2. Pen or pencil
3. Treasure Map on the book of Philippians on pages 155-160

Directions for Diggers

When you see people having a really hard time, do you wonder why life has such tough times?

This week we are going to talk about one of the tough times in Paul's life and see truth treasures in God's Word that made the difference for him when he suffered.

God wants you to be strong when tough times come, and He wants to show you truths that will help you just like they helped Paul.

Why don't you stop and pray right now. Ask God to help you see how tough times can really be good times. Pray that you'll discover why you can rejoice—be happy—even in bad times. Ask Him to help you understand how suffering can be used to make you more like Jesus.

LAYER ONE: When Things Go Wrong

1. Does being a Christian mean that you will never suffer? Does it mean that everything will always go smoothly? Does being a Christian mean that you'll never be hurt? If you are a Christian, does this mean that you'll never be disappointed?

    a. Dig out Philippians 1:29 from your "Treasure Map" and write it out below.

    b. What did you learn about suffering from the verse you wrote out? Will a Christian ever suffer?

    c. Read John 15:18-21. See if you can discover why a Christian should expect to suffer. Write your answer below the verses.

18 "If the world hates you, you know that it has hated Me before *it hated* you. **19** "If you were of the world, the world would love its own; but because you are not of the world, but I chose you out of the world, because of this the world hates you. **20** "Remember the word that I said to you, 'A slave is not greater than his master.' If they persecuted Me, they will also persecute you; if they kept My word, they will keep yours also. **21** "But all these things they will do to you for My name's sake, because they do not know the One who sent Me.

2. When Paul wrote this book to the Philippians, he was suffering. Let's see what we can discover about Paul's suffering.

    a. In Philippians 1:29, we discover that Christians will suffer. Go back to the "Treasure Map" in the back of your book and use your red colored pencil to make a large "S" over the word *suffer* in this verse.

Do you remember where Paul was when he wrote this letter? That's right. In Dig Two, we learned that he was in prison.

Paul was in prison because he was telling people about the Lord Jesus Christ. The officials were upset because Paul's beliefs went against the religion of the day. They felt that he threatened how they had always done things.

But because Paul knew what Jesus had done for him while he was a sinner, he wanted others to know too. Paul would not be silent about Jesus, so they put him in prison.

b. Turn to Philippians 1:12-19 on your "Treasure Map." When you see that Paul's suffering was to be in prison for telling people about Jesus, mark the word *imprisonment* the same way you marked the word *suffer*—with a large "S."

c. Since Paul's "circumstances" were being in prison, look at Philippians 1:12 and mark the word *circumstances* the same way you marked *suffer* and *imprisonment*.

d. Dig through Philippians 1:12-18 again on your "Treasure Map." This time, make a list below of what you uncover about Paul's imprisonment and suffering. Remember that lists help you pull a bunch of ideas about something together so that you can see them easily.

You can be sure your list is complete by looking at each of the words you marked with an "S" and noting what you learn. Take your time and make each point as short as you can. Tomorrow we will use this list to answer some questions about suffering.

Paul's Suffering

1.

2.

3.

4.

5.

6.

7.

8.

9.

Do you love the Lord so much that even though it's hard, you tell your friends about Him anyway? Remember that everyone needs to know about Jesus so that they have the chance to let Him save them too. When you are afraid to tell others about Jesus, think of how brave Paul was! And think about how many people came to know Jesus because he was so brave!

LAYER TWO: How Can I Be Strong?

Are you ready for another day of digging? Great! Let's get started.

1. Read Philippians 1:12-18 again. Review the list of treasures you discovered yesterday about Paul's imprisonment and suffering.

    a. Why was Paul in prison (verse 13)?

    b. What did his circumstances (imprisonment) result in (verse 12)?

2. You saw that Paul's imprisonment and suffering was because he preached the gospel. Let's see if we can understand this gospel that Paul believed in so strongly.

    a. The gospel is defined in 1 Corinthians 15:1-5. Observe these verses.

1 Now I make known to you, brethren, the gospel which I preached to you, which also you received, in which you also stand, **2** by which also you are saved, if you hold fast the word which I preached to you, unless you believed in vain. **3** For I delivered to you as of first importance what I also received, that Christ died for our sins according to the Scriptures, **4** and that He was buried, and that He was raised on the third day according to the Scriptures, **5** and that He appeared to Cephas, then to the twelve.

    b. Now I'll help you uncover the major points of the gospel from the verses above. **Clue #9:** You are looking for four points. They begin in verse 3. Each one begins with the word *that*.
        See if you can dig out the four points or truths that tell the gospel of Christ and list them below. Another list!

that

that

that

that

(This fourth truth is important because it proved that Jesus had been raised from the dead!)

3. Now let's see if we can discover why Paul was willing to suffer imprisonment for the gospel.

a. Read Romans 1:16 and then write it out below.

b. From what you see in Romans 1:16 above, why is the gospel so important?

This verse may be difficult for you to understand, but it means that God uses the gospel to save people from their sins. The gospel is powerful because it contains the truth that can save people!

Can you see why Paul was willing to suffer for people to know the gospel?

4. Philippians 1:12 mentions the "progress of the gospel." What does the word "progress" mean? **Clue #10:** You might think of it like this: You have been given the job of painting a large room. Every day after school, you go to the room for a couple of hours and spread paint on the wall. Each day more and more of the wall is covered with paint. You're making progress!

What do you think Paul meant when he said that the gospel was making progress?

You're doing well. Don't get tired of digging. I know some of the truths you're uncovering are hard to dig out and understand, but they are very important. I trust you'll hang in there with me. I want you to become a Master Digger, and you are on your way!

And I want you to really understand what the gospel is. And I want to be sure you can see why we should all be willing to suffer so that others can hear it.

LAYER THREE: With the Courage of a Lion

Yesterday we saw that Paul was in prison and that this caused the gospel to spread. If Paul was confined to prison, he was not free to move around and preach and talk to people. Then how could that cause the gospel to spread?

1. Dig through Philippians 1:12-14 again.

2. The word "brethren" in verse 14 is talking about other Christians. What did they do when they saw what happened to Paul?

One of my good animal friends is a lion, Leo. Lions have a lot of courage. You know they're the king of the jungle! If something big and scary comes their way, they don't run away and hide. These Christians had courage like a lion. They saw Paul being courageous and standing up for what he believed, even if he had to go to prison. It made them want to do the same thing. See how Paul's suffering was used in the lives of others!

3. Verse 13 tells us that someone else heard about Paul's imprisonment. Who was it?

The praetorian guard are the men who guarded the prisoners. So even the prison guards heard about Paul and his belief in Jesus Christ because of his imprisonment.

4. Paul goes on to talk about how the gospel is being spread. Then in verse 18 he tells us how he felt about his circumstances. Read verse 18 and write how he felt.

Paul's goal in life was to tell people about Jesus so that they could be set free from sin—just like he was. Since being in prison was resulting in more people knowing about the gospel, he was happy. Even though the circumstances were hard, Paul looked past the prison walls to see what God was doing! He rejoiced in that.

Sometimes we need to think about the fact that even though things are hard, God can use the hard times to do great things.

5. Dig out Romans 8:28 in your Bible, and write it out below.

This verse shows us that God causes all things to work for good—even the hard things or the bad things that we don't understand. This doesn't mean all things are good; they aren't. But it does mean that God can use even the bad things to accomplish something good. He was able to use Paul's imprisonment to cause many people to hear the gospel.

Because this is true, we can rejoice—be content—in all things. God is in control. Therefore, we can rejoice.

LAYER FOUR: If We Obey Him

Yesterday we saw that Paul could rejoice even while he was in prison because God was using his imprisonment to spread the gospel.

We also looked at Romans 8:28 which told us that God causes all things to work together for good—not just for Paul but for us also.

However, there is a fact that we must not overlook. Even though God is in control and even though He causes all things to work for good, we have a responsibility.

What do I mean by that? Well, I mean there are some things we must do also. Let's talk about it more today.

1. Observe Romans 8:28 again. (Remember, you wrote it out in yesterday's lesson.) If God is to work all things together for good, there is something you must do. What is it?

2. Again, why was Paul in prison? Had he done something wrong?

3. Dig out Philippians 1:19-20 and read it carefully. This scripture tells us that Paul knows that God will work out his imprisonment for good. It goes on to tell us what Paul's expectation and hope (the thing he desires most) is. What is it?

Fill in the spaces by looking at these verses to find out.

According to my earnest expectation and hope, that I _____ ____

____ _____ _____ _____ in anything, but that with all boldness,

_____ _____ _____ _____ as always, _____ _____

_____ _____ _____ , whether by life or by death.

4. So we see from these scriptures that we can expect God to work all things for good *if* we suffer for Him. Our responsibility is to love God and obey Him—that's our part!

You've found some great treasures, haven't you? We'll discover more tomorrow.

LAYER FIVE: Everyone Suffers

Let's look at some other scriptures which tell us more about suffering. You'll see that you may suffer for doing what is right or for doing what is wrong. When you do suffer for loving God and being obedient, He will help you through it all!

1. Dig into 1 Peter 3:14, 16-17 and answer the questions that follow.

> **14** But even if you should suffer for the sake of righteous, *you are* blessed.... **16** and keep a good conscience so that in the thing in which you are slandered, those who revile your good behavior in Christ will be put to shame. **17** For it is better, if God should will it so, that you suffer for doing what is right rather than for doing what is wrong.

   a. What brings blessing?

   b. If we do what is right (keep a good conscience), how will it affect those who make fun of us?

   c. What does verse 17 say is better?

2. Dig into 1 Peter 4:14-16 now and then answer a few more questions. You're really getting close to some precious stones of truth now!

> **14** If you are reviled for the name of Christ, you are blessed, because the Spirit of glory and of God rests on you. **15** Make sure that none of you suffers as a murderer, or thief, or evildoer, or a troublesome meddler; **16** but if *anyone suffers* as a Christian, he is not to be ashamed, but is to glorify God in this name.

   a. If you are reviled for the name of Christ, what are you? **Clue #11:** Revile means to use abusive language. It means someone talks mean or ugly to you.

   b. What does it mean to be blessed? Write what you think, and then I'll tell you what I think.

I think blessed means to be honored. If God sees that we are suffering for doing what is right, He blesses us. He honors us. He knows we are loving Him and doing what He has asked, and He makes all of what happens work out for our good. It may take a while, but He will do it!

    c. You can also suffer for doing wrong. In the verses in 1 Peter 4, you see a list of people who suffer for doing wrong. List them below.

Do you understand that if you are any of these things, you would be disobedient to what God wants? Then He could not honor you.

    d. Look above at 1 Peter 4:16. If you are a Christian, how are you to respond to suffering?

3. Let's review what we have learned this week about suffering. You now have some more precious stones to add to your chest of truths!

Stone 1—Christians will suffer. Their suffering should not be the result of their own disobedience.

Stone 2— Christians can rejoice in their suffering because God will cause all things to work together for good.

Stone 3—We saw this second stone of truth played out in Paul's suffering. Although he had done nothing wrong, he was in prison. However, he was rejoicing because his imprisonment meant that many people heard the gospel.

So if you are obedient and you still suffer, you can rejoice in your suffering. First you can rejoice because God is in control. You can also rejoice because you know He will work it all out for good! You can know you are blessed!

4. Being in prison is not the only way Christians can suffer. List some ways that you as a Christian young person might have to suffer.

Ask God to give you the courage to ALWAYS do what is right and what will honor Him. You know, don't you, that because you're spending time in the Word of God, you'll know what is right? And since you know what is right, God will expect you to do it. That's a BIG responsibility. And I'm proud of you for wanting to know the truth and for spending the time to dig it out!

**Take some time to do one of your favorite things now that your work is done.
I'm off to do the same.**

TRUTH TREASURES FOR THE WEEK

1.

2.

3.

BURY THE TREASURE:

For to you it has been granted for Christ's sake, not only to believe in Him, but also to suffer for His sake (Philippians 1:29).

Dig 7

Joseph—A Kid Who Conquered!

Tools of the Trade

1. Colored pencils
2. Pen or pencil
3. Key Word Puzzle on page 94

Directions for Diggers

This week we're going to talk a little more about the topic of suffering. And I want to introduce you to another friend of mine. I think you'll enjoy meeting him just as much as you enjoyed meeting Paul a few days ago. Joseph is also a Master Digger! He loved the truth and lived it.

I want you to meet this friend because he is a good example of a young person who suffered lots. He is also a good example of someone who understood that God was in control. He trusted God—even when he couldn't understand all that was happening to him.

Hope you're ready for a great week of digging together! Ask God to use the story of Joseph to show you how to handle tough times.

This dig may seem long, but it's because I have included the verses for you to read. So hang in there. Don't get discouraged. This story of Joseph is one of the best in the Bible—and it's full of truth treasures for you to discover!

Special Find: You're going to read a lot this week about a guy called Pharaoh. You may know all about the Pharaohs because you may have studied about them in school. But in case you haven't, I wanted to tell you that it is a title for a man who held the office of the top ruler in Egypt—sort of like the President of the United States.

Okay, now let's get started.

LAYER ONE: A Surprising Story

1. You may already know Joseph, but if not, I am excited to introduce you to him. His story is in the book of Genesis. The story begins in Genesis 37. Read Genesis 37:1-11.

> **1** Now Jacob lived in the land where his father had soujourned, in the land of Canaan. **2** These are *the records of* the generations of Jacob. Joseph, when seventeen years of age, was pasturing the flock with his brothers while he was *still* a youth, along with the sons of Bilhah and the sons of Zilpah, his father's wives. And Joseph brought back a bad report about them to their father. **3** Now Israel loved Joseph more than all his sons, because he was the son of his old age; and he made him a varicolored tunic. **4** His brothers saw that their father loved him more than all his brothers; and *so* they hated him and could not speak to him on friendly terms. **5** Then Joseph had a dream, and when he told it to his brothers, they hated him even more. **6** He said to them, "Please listen to this dream which I have had; **7** for behold, we were binding sheaves in the field, and lo, my sheaf rose up and also stood erect; and behold, your sheaves gathered around and bowed down to my sheaf." **8** Then his brothers said to him, "Are you actually going to reign over us? Or are you really going to rule over us?" So they hated him even more for his dreams and for his words. **9** Now he had still another dream, and related it to his brothers, and said, "Lo, I have had still another dream; and behold, the sun and the moon and eleven stars were bowing down to me." **10** He related *it* to his father and to his brothers; and his father rebuked him and said to him, "What is this dream that you have had? Shall I and your mother and your brothers actually come to bow ourselves down before you to the ground?" **11** His brothers were jealous of him, but his father kept the saying *in mind*.

a. Why did Joseph's brothers hate him? If you don't remember, look at verses 4-5 again.

b. Read verse 11 and write down another feeling his brothers had toward him.

2. Now read Genesis 37:12-28.

12 Then his brothers went to pasture their father's flocks in Shechem. **13** Israel said to Joseph, "Are not your brothers pasturing *the flock* in Shechem? Come, and I will send you to them." And he said to him, "I will go." **14** Then he said to him, "Go now and see about the welfare of the flock, and bring word back to me." So he sent him from the valley of Hebron, and he came to Shechem. **15** A man found him, and behold, he was wandering in the field; and the man asked him, "What are you looking for?" **16** He said, "I am looking for my brothers; please tell me where they are pasturing *the flock*." **17** Then the man said, "They have moved from here; for I heard *them* say, 'Let us go to Dothan.'" So Joseph went after his brothers and found them at Dothan. **18** When they saw him from a distance and before he came close to them, they plotted against him to put him to death. **19** They said to one another, "Here comes this dreamer! **20** "Now then, come and let us kill him and throw him into one of the pits; and we will say, 'A wild beast devoured him.' Then let us see what will become of his dreams!" **21** But Reuben heard *this* and rescued him out of their hands and said, "Let us not take his life." **22** Reuben further said to them, "Shed no blood. Throw him into this pit that is in the wilderness, but do not lay hands on him"—that he might rescue him out of their hands, to restore him to his father. **23** So it came about, when Joseph reached his brothers, that they stripped Joseph of his tunic, the varicolored tunic that was on him; **24** and they took him and threw him into the pit. Now the pit was empty, without any water in it. **25** Then they sat down to eat

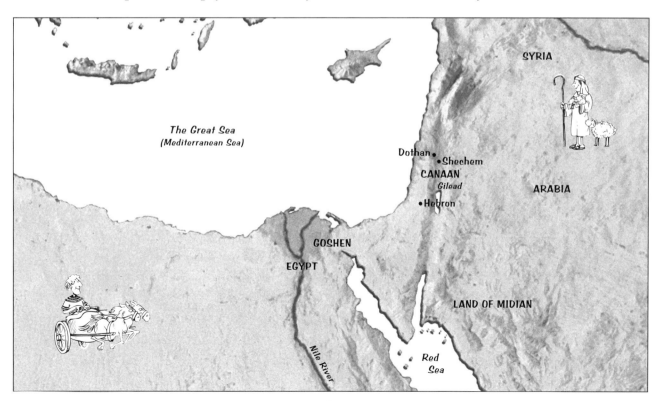

a meal. And as they raised their eyes and looked, behold, a caravan of Ishmaelites was coming from Gilead, with their camels bearing aromatic gum and balm and myrrh, on their way to bring *them* down to Egypt. **26** Judah said to his brothers, "What profit is it for us to kill our brother and cover up his blood? **27** "Come and let us sell him to the Ishmaelites and not lay our hands on him, for he is our brother, our *own* flesh." And his brothers listened *to him*. **28** Then some Midianite traders passed by, so they pulled *him* up and lifted Joseph out of the pit, and sold him to the Ishmaelites for twenty *shekels* of silver. Thus they brought Joseph into Egypt.

a. Joseph's dad sent him to check on his brothers. What did they do when they saw him coming? Read verses 18-20 again.

b. Reuben, one of his brothers, couldn't go through with the plan. Read verses 21-22 to see what Reuben suggested. What was it?

c. What did the brothers do?

3. In verses 26-27, Judah suggested a plan, and the brothers followed it. What did they do?

4. Let's read more of the story. Read verses 29-36 and then answer the questions that follow.

29 Now Reuben returned to the pit, and behold, Joseph was not in the pit; so he tore his garments. **30** He returned to his brothers and said, "The boy is not *there*; as for me, where am I to go?" **31** So they took Joseph's tunic, and slaughtered a male goat and dipped the tunic in the blood; **32** and they sent the varicolored tunic and brought it to their father and said, "We found this; please examine it to *see* whether it is your son's tunic or not." **33** Then he examined *it* and said, "It is my son's tunic. A wild beast has devoured him; Joseph has surely been torn to pieces!" **34** So Jacob tore his clothes, and put sackcloth on his loins and mourned for his son many days. **35** Then all his sons and all his daughters arose to comfort him, but he refused to be comforted. And he said, "Surely I will go down to Sheol in mourning for my son." So his father wept for him. **36** Meanwhile, the Midianites sold him in Egypt to Potiphar, Pharaoh's officer, the captain of the bodyguard.

a. What did the brothers do to try to hide what they had done?

b. Did their father believe that Joseph was dead?

5. Read verse 36. What happened to Joseph?

It would be pretty bad to have your family hate you so much that they wanted you dead or gone, wouldn't it? I'd call that suffering!

Many things, good and bad, happened to Joseph while he was in Egypt. The rest of this week, we're going to look at the way God used all of what happened for Joseph's good AND for the good of his family.

Did you see the mention of my family in verse 25? I told you that my ancestors were hanging around when all of the action of the Old Testament happened!

Catch you tomorrow.

LAYER TWO: Where Is God When I Hurt?

As we begin today, remember that God is in charge. Remember, too, that He will take the things that make you suffer and use them for your good. Sometimes it may take a long time to see what good comes out of suffering, but God will keep His promise and use your circumstances for your good.

Yesterday we saw Joseph sold into slavery by his brothers. If you had been Joseph, how would you have felt? Would you have been angry? Would you have wanted to get even? Or would you have been afraid and hurt? Let's see what Joseph did.

1. Read Genesis 39:1-6.

> **1** Now Joseph had been taken down to Egypt; and Potiphar, an Egyptian officer of Pharaoh, the captain of the bodyguard, bought him from the Ishmaelites, who had taken him down there. **2** The Lord was with Joseph, so he became a successful man. And he was in the house of his master, the Egyptian. **3** Now his master saw that the Lord was with him and *how* the Lord caused all that he did to prosper in his hand. **4** So Joseph found favor in his sight and became his personal servant; and he made him overseer over his house, and all that he owned he put in his charge. **5** It came about that from the time he made him overseer in his house and over all that he owned, the Lord blessed the Egyptian's house on account of Joseph; thus the Lord's blessing was upon all that he owned, in the house and in the field. **6** So he left

everything he owned in Joseph's charge; and with him *there* he did not concern himself with anything except the food which he ate. Now Joseph was handsome in form and appearance.

a. Once Joseph was in Egypt, how were things going for him?

b. Take a colored pencil and mark the word *Lord* every time you see it in the verses above, by making a cross:

c. From what you just saw by marking the word *Lord*, who do you think was in charge of all that was happening?

It looks like God is beginning to work Joseph's circumstances out for good, doesn't it?

2. Next let's read Genesis 39:7-20. Hang in there. You're going to really like this story.

7 It came about after these events that his master's wife looked with desire at Joseph, and she said, "Lie with me." **8** But he refused and said to his master's wife, "Behold, with me *here*, my master does not concern himself with anything in the house, and he has put all that he owns in my charge. **9** "There is no one greater in this house than I, and he has withheld nothing from me except you, because you are his wife. How then could I do this great evil and sin against God?" **10** As she spoke to Joseph day after day, he did not listen to her to lie beside her *or* be with her. **11** Now it happened one day that he went into the house to do his work, and none of the men of the household was there inside. **12** She caught him by his garment, saying, "Lie with me!" And he left his garment in her hand and fled, and went outside. **13** When she saw that he had left his garment in her hand and had fled outside, **14** she called to the men of her household and said to them, "See, he has brought in a Hebrew to us to make sport of us; he came in to me to lie with me, and I screamed. **15** "When he heard that I raised my voice and screamed, he left his garment beside me and fled and went outside." **16** So she left his garment beside her until his master came home. **17** Then she spoke to him with these words, "The Hebrew slave, whom you brought to us, came in to me to make sport of me; **18** and as I raised my voice and screamed, he left his garment beside me and fled outside." **19** Now when his master heard the words of his wife, which she spoke to him, saying, "This is what your slave did to me," his anger burned. **20** So Joseph's master took him and put him into the jail, the place where the king's prisoners were confined; and he was there in the jail.

a. Did Joseph do anything wrong?

b. Did he do anything right?

c. Where did Joseph end up?

d. Was that fair?

e. Does all of this mean that God was no longer in control?

4. Now take a look at Genesis 39:21-23.

21 But the Lord was with Joseph and extended kindness to him, and gave him favor in the sight of the chief jailer. **22** The chief jailer committed to Joseph's charge all the prisoners who were in the jail; so that whatever was done there, he was responsible *for it*. **23** The chief jailer did not supervise anything under Joseph's charge because the Lord was with him; and whatever he did, the Lord made to prosper.

a. Again, mark the word *Lord* and see who was in control. Who was in charge?

b. What happened to Joseph?

5. Continue on with the story by reading Genesis 40:1-14, then answer the questions that follow.

1 Then it came about after these things, the cupbearer and the baker for the king of Egypt offended their lord, the king of Egypt. **2** Pharaoh was furious with his two officials, the chief cupbearer and the chief baker. **3** So he put them in confinement in the house of the captain of the bodyguard, in the jail, the *same* place where Joseph was imprisoned. **4** The captain of the bodyguard put Joseph in charge of them, and he took care of them; and they were in confinement for some time. **5** Then the cupbearer and the baker for the king of Egypt, who were confined in jail, both had a dream the same night, each man with his *own* dream *and* each dream with its *own* interpretation. **6** When Joseph came to them in the morning and observed them, behold, they were dejected. **7** He asked Pharaoh's officials who were with him in confinement in his master's house, "Why are your faces so sad today?" **8** Then they said to him, "We have had a dream and there is no one to interpret it." Then Joseph said to them, "Do not interpretations belong to God? Tell *it* to me, please." **9** So the chief cupbearer told his dream to Joseph, and said to him, "In my dream, behold, *there was* a vine in front of me; **10** and on the vine *were* three branches. And as it was budding, its blossoms came out, *and* its clusters produced ripe grapes. **11** "Now Pharaoh's cup was in my hand; so I took the grapes and squeezed them into Pharaoh's cup, and I put the cup into Pharaoh's hand." **12** Then Joseph said to him, "This is the interpretation of it: the three branches are three days; **13** within three more days Pharaoh will lift up your head and restore you to your office; and you will put Pharaoh's cup into his hand according to your former custom when you were his cupbearer. **14** "Only keep me in mind when it goes well with you, and please do me a kindness by mentioning me to Pharaoh and get me out of this house."

a. What did Joseph do for the cupbearer? (If you want to know about the baker, you can read the rest of the chapter in your Bible.)

b. What did Joseph ask the cupbearer to do?

Let's skip to the end of the chapter and read one verse to see if the cupbearer did what Joseph asked.

23 Yet the chief cupbearer did not remember Joseph, but forgot him.

It's sort of hard to believe how things keep going wrong for Joseph, isn't it? Imagine being able to ask God to help you understand the dreams of these men and then actually being able to know what the dreams mean! All Joseph asked for in return was that the cupbearer would tell the Pharaoh about him, and the guy forgot!

Just remember that God was in charge the entire time. Sometimes it gets hard to believe that when things keep going wrong, but wait until the end of the story!

LAYER THREE: From a Prison to a Palace

Today there is more Scripture to read, but aren't you having fun learning about Joseph and about how God worked in his life? I am very excited when I think about how God wants to work in your life! I know Joseph is a great example for you! Let's read more!

1. Let's begin in Genesis 41:1-14.

1 Now it happened at the end of two full years that Pharaoh had a dream, and behold, he was standing by the Nile. **2** And lo, from the Nile there came up seven cows, sleek and fat; and they grazed in the marsh grass. **3** Then behold, seven other cows came up after them from the Nile, ugly and gaunt, and they stood by the *other* cows on the bank of the Nile. **4** The ugly and gaunt cows ate up the seven sleek and fat cows. Then Pharaoh awoke. **5** He fell asleep and dreamed a second time; and behold, seven ears of grain came up on a single stalk, plump and good. **6** Then behold, seven ears, thin and scorched by the east wind, sprouted up after them. **7** The thin ears swallowed up the seven plump and full ears. Then Pharaoh awoke, and behold, *it was* a dream. **8** Now in the morning his spirit was troubled, so he sent and called for all the magicians of Egypt, and all its wise men. And Pharaoh told them his dreams, but there was no one who could interpret them to Pharaoh. **9** Then the chief cupbearer spoke to Pharaoh, saying, "I would make mention today of my *own* offenses. **10** "Pharaoh was furious with his servants and he put me in confinement in the house of captain of the bodyguard, *both* me and the chief baker. **11** "We had a dream on the same night, he and I; each of us dreamed according to the interpretation of his *own* dream. **12** "Now a Hebrew youth *was* with us there, a servant of the captain of the bodyguard, and we related *them* to him, and he interpreted dreams for us. To each one he interpreted according to his *own* dream. **13** "And just as he interpreted for us, so it happened; he restored me in my office, but he hanged him." **14** Then Pharaoh sent and called for Joseph, and they hurriedly brought him out of the dungeon; and when he had shaved himself and changed his clothes, he came to Pharaoh.

a. How many years had passed?

b. What happened to cause the cupbearer to remember Joseph?

2. Next in chapter 41, Joseph is brought to Pharaoh and told about his dreams. Just as before, God helped Joseph explain what the dreams meant—that there were to be seven years of plenty then seven years of famine. Let's read more of the story from Genesis 41.

39 So Pharaoh said to Joseph, "Since God has informed you of all this, there is no one so discerning and wise as you are. **40** "You shall be over my house, and according to your command all my people shall do homage; only in the throne I will be greater than you." **41** Pharaoh said to Joseph, "See, I have set you over all the land of Egypt." **42** Then Pharaoh took off his signet ring from his hand and put it on Joseph's hand, and clothed him in garments of fine linen and put the gold necklace around his neck. **43** He had him ride in his second chariot; and they proclaimed before him, "Bow the knee!" And he set him over all the land of Egypt. **44** Moreover, Pharaoh said to Joseph, *"Though* I am Pharaoh, yet without your permission no one shall raise his hand or foot in all the land of Egypt." **45** Then Pharaoh named Joseph Zaphenathpaneah; and he gave him Asenath, the daughter of Potiphera priest of On, as his wife. And Joseph went forth over the land of Egypt.... **47** During the seven years of plenty the land brought forth abundantly. **48** So he gathered all the food of *these* seven years which occurred in the land of Egypt and placed the food in the cities; he placed in every city the food from its own surrounding fields. **49** Thus Joseph stored up grain in great abundance like the sand of the sea, until he stopped measuring *it*, for it was beyond measure. **50** Now before the year of famine came, two sons were born to Joseph....

a. What did Pharaoh do for Joseph?

b. What did Joseph do once he was in this new position? Why did he do it?

3. Now read the end of Genesis 41.

53 When the seven years of plenty which had been in the land of Egypt came to an end, **54** and the seven years of famine began to come, just as Joseph had said, then there was famine in all the lands, but in all the land of Egypt there was bread. **55** So when all the land of Egypt was famished, the people cried out to Pharaoh for bread; and Pharaoh said to all the Egyptians, "Go to Joseph; whatever he says to you, you shall do." **56** When the famine was *spread* over all the face of the earth, then Joseph opened all the storehouses, and sold to the Egyptians; and the famine was severe in the land of Egypt. **57** *The people of* all the earth came to Egypt to buy grain from Joseph, because the famine was severe in all the earth.

a. Did God do what He said He would do through Pharaoh's dreams?

b. How widespread was the famine?

Are you beginning to see how God is in control even when we can't see that He is? Think about Joseph's circumstances and think now of where he is—the second in command of all Egypt.

Let's take a break and finish the story tomorrow in Layer Four. See you then.

LAYER FOUR: God Meant It for Good!

1. Now for the rest of the story. Read Genesis 42:1-3.

> **1** Now Jacob saw that there was grain in Egypt, and Jacob said to his sons, "Why are you staring at one another?" **2** He said, "Behold, I have heard that there is grain in Egypt; go down there and buy *some* for us from that place, so that we may live and not die." **3** Then ten brothers of Joseph went down to buy grain from Egypt.

2. When the brothers went to Egypt to buy grain, it was necessary for them to appear before Joseph. When they bowed before him, he recognized them and remembered the dreams he had when he was a young boy. (You read about those dreams in Layer One.) However, the brothers did not recognize Joseph.

Joseph had them thrown into jail as spies. He later heard them expressing their sorrow for having sold him into slavery. Then he came up with a plan. He ordered that one of the brothers be held in prison and that the other nine go home and bring back the youngest brother. The youngest brother, Benjamin, had stayed at home with Jacob, his father.

Jacob was so grieved by the loss of Joseph, and now he thought he had lost another son to a prison in Egypt! He refused to allow the youngest brother to return to Egypt with his brother. He did not want to lose him too!

The famine got worse. So finally Jacob was forced to allow Benjamin to return to Egypt with the others. They needed food! Joseph was greatly touched by the sight of Benjamin. He brought the brothers into his own house and fed them.

Then Joseph had another plan. He ordered his servant to fill their sacks with grain and to place his silver cup in Benjamin's sack. Finally the brothers left for home. On their way back, the brothers were stopped by Joseph's men. These men accused them of stealing. When the sacks were searched, they found the cup in Benjamin's sack.

Judah was very upset. He had promised his father he would bring Benjamin home unharmed. So he plead with Joseph for mercy. He told him how sad their father would be if he lost another son.

3. Read Genesis 45:1-11.

1 Then Joseph could not control himself before all those who stood by him, and he cried, "Have everyone go out from me." So there was no man with him when Joseph made himself known to his brothers. **2** He wept so loudly that the Egyptians heard *it*, and the household of Pharaoh heard of *it*. **3** Then Joseph said to his brothers, "I am Joseph! Is my father still alive?" But his brothers could not answer him, for they were dismayed at his presence. **4** Then Joseph said to his brothers, "Please come closer to me." And they came closer. And he said, "I am your brother Joseph, whom you sold into Egypt. **5** "Now do not be grieved or angry with yourselves, because you sold me here, for God sent me before you to preserve life. **6** "For the famine *has been* in the land these two years, and there are still five years in which there will be neither plowing nor harvesting. **7** "God sent me before you to preserve for you a remnant in the earth, and to keep you alive by a great deliverance. **8** "Now, therefore, it was not you who sent me here, but God; and He has made me a father to Pharaoh and lord of all his household and ruler over all the land of Egypt. **9** "Hurry and go up to my father, and say to him, 'Thus says your son Joseph, "God has made me lord of all Egypt; come down to me, do not delay. **10** "You shall live in the land of Goshen, and you shall be near me, you and your children and your children's children and your flocks and your herds and all that you have. **11** "There I will also provide for you, for there are still five years of famine *to come*, and you and your household and all that you have would be impoverished."'

a. Did Joseph hold a grudge against his brothers for what they had done to him?

b. Who did Joseph say sent him to Egypt?

c. How did God cause all the circumstances to work for good for Joseph?

d. How did God cause all the circumstances to work for good for Joseph's family?

e. Who was in control of all that happened to Joseph?

4. If you'll always remember that God is in control, it will help you be content in your circumstances. *This is one of the greatest truth treasures in the whole Bible!*

You'd think Joseph might have wanted to get even with his brothers, wouldn't you? Take your Bible and read what he said in Genesis 50:20. Write it below.

If Joseph had not been in Egypt, his family wouldn't have had grain and would have died of hunger. God knew all that would happen, and Joseph's suffering made a way for his family to be protected!

5. What can you learn from this story that will help you when you suffer because of what someone else does to you?

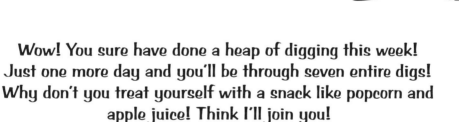

Wow! You sure have done a heap of digging this week!
Just one more day and you'll be through seven entire digs!
Why don't you treat yourself with a snack like popcorn and
apple juice! Think I'll join you!

LAYER FIVE: Joyful in All Things

By now you've seen that being a Christian does not keep us from suffering. As a matter of fact, being a Christian and obeying God will probably bring suffering. We have looked at the suffering of Paul and Joseph and seen how God caused their circumstances to work for good.

We also saw last week that being put in prison is not the only way we might suffer. It hurts very much when our friends or family make fun of us for obeying God, and it is very tempting to go along with the crowd so they won't laugh at us.

But how are we to respond to the suffering we might experience? Let's talk about that today.

1. How did Joseph respond to his circumstances? Did he hold a grudge and try to get even?

2. How did Paul respond to his imprisonment? If you need a reminder, read Philippians 1:18.

3. As we finish our study on suffering, let's look at two last scriptures that will help us know how to respond when we suffer. Read these verses and answer a couple of questions—and then you'll be at the bottom of Layer Five and all done digging for the week!

   a. Read James 1:2-3.

    2 Consider it all joy, my brethren, when you encounter trials, **3** knowing that the testing of your faith produces endurance.

      (1) How are you to respond when you hit tough times?

      (2) Can you see why you can feel this way?

      (3) What is endurance? Why is it important? You may need someone to help you with this question, but that's okay!

   b. Read 1 Peter 4:12-14

    12 Beloved, do not be surprised at the firey ordeal among you, which comes upon you for your testing, as though some strange thing were happening to you; **13** but to the degree that you share the sufferings of Christ, keep on rejoicing, so that also at the revelation of His glory you may rejoice in exultation. **14** If you are reviled for the name of Christ, you are blessed, because the Spirit of glory and of God rests on you.

      (1) Do you think it is normal for a Christian to have some trials, some tough times, some things that cause him or her to suffer?

      (2) When hard times come along, how are you to respond?

(3) Why can you respond that way? What rests upon you that makes it possible?

4. The next time you find yourself in bad circumstances or having a hard time and you didn't do anything wrong, should you get angry for what went wrong? Why not?

5. What should you do the next time you go through hard times or pressures?

We've unearthed lots of treasures about suffering in these last couple of digs, haven't we? Ask the Lord to help you remember all that you've learned so that next time a difficult circumstance comes, you'll be ready!

Why don't you have some fun with the puzzle on page 94 before you stop for the week? See you next week.

TRUTH TREASURES FOR THE WEEK

1.

2.

3.

BURY THE TREASURE:

And we know that God causes all things to work together for good to those who love God, to those who are called according to the *His* purpose (Romans 8:28).

KEY WORD PUZZLE

1 Six words are hidden in the pyramid.

2 To solve the puzzle, think back through this lesson to people and things we have talked about. Unscramble each word and write it on the space below the scrambled letters.

3 Once you have all of the words unscrambled, look at each line and find the letter inside the (parenthesis). Take each of these letters and fill in the (parentheses) of the first line under "New Name Scramble."

4 Now, see if you can unscramble this name on the second line under "New Name Scramble."

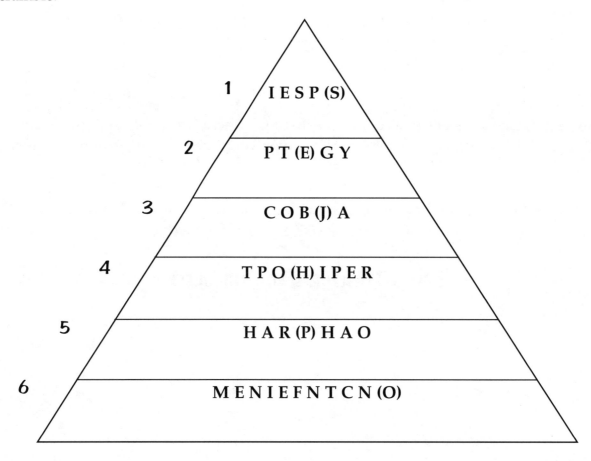

NEW NAME SCRAMBLE

(__) (__) (__) (__) (__) (__)

— — — — — —

Dig 8

Jesus, Our Great Treasure!

Tools of the Trade

1. Colored pencils
2. Pen or pencil
3. Treasure Map on the book of Philippians on pages 155-160

Directions for Diggers

Well, you've learned a lot about suffering in the last couple of digs, haven't you? I hope that one of the main things you'll remember is that when Christians find themselves in difficult circumstances or hard times, they are told to rejoice.

Do you remember why Christians can rejoice or be content even in tough times? If you said because God is in charge, you're right! That really makes all the difference, doesn't it?

It's like going to bed and sleeping soundly all through the night because you know your parents are in the house. You know they'll take care of anything that could hurt you. You're safe and secure in God's care too. You can always know He will take care of you even when you can't see how! Now, that's a reason to rejoice!

This week's lesson is a very, very important one. You should ask your mom or dad to review each day's work with you after you finish. It's really important that you understand all that you study, and some of the ideas are very adult ideas. I know you can do it, though, because you're such a great Bible student. Let's get going!

LAYER ONE: A Walk That's Worthy

After Paul talks about suffering, he tells the Philippians that they will suffer, too, for Christ's sake. Next, Paul talks about acting "worthy." In other words, whether they have tough times or everything is good, he wants them to remember what they know about God and act like they know it! He calls this kind of behavior *conducting yourself in a manner worthy of the gospel.*

Do you know what it means to be worthy? **Clue #12:** Think about when your parents ask you to take out the trash, mow the grass, wash the dishes, or clean your room…and you do! Then, even though you didn't know they planned to, they take you out for ice cream as a reward. You're worthy because you did what you were asked to do. You didn't think that you'd get anything for it. You did it because God says to obey your parents.

Worthy means that you deserve something.

1. First let's look at some things Paul says to the Philippians about why he thinks they should walk worthy. Here's how we'll begin: Turn to Philippians 2:1-2 on your "Treasure Map" and read these verses. As you read, use a colored pencil and draw a circle around the word *if*.

2. In the verses you read, the word *if* means *because*. Now let's write out what Paul says in these verses, and let's substitute the word *because* for the word *if*. I'll help you:

Walk Worthy:

BECAUSE there is e _____ in Christ

BECAUSE there is l _____

BECAUSE there is f _____

BECAUSE there is _____ and _____

We see that in Christ we have encouragement, love, fellowship, and affection and compassion. Those are all *BIG* things! And we have them all in Christ. Paul wants us to *walk worthy* of them, to act like we deserve them!

3. What do these things mean? Why don't you try to explain the first two, and I'll do the last three.
   a. Can you think of a way to define *encouragement*? Has someone encouraged you lately? Give it a try.

I think of encouragement when I think of how I felt when I couldn't get all of these lessons written for you. My friend kept on telling me I could do it. She tried to help me find a quiet place to write. She also tried to help by doing other things that I would normally do so that I could have more time to write. She encouraged me!

    b. I know you can define love. Go for it!

It is neat to think about the kind of love we have in Christ. When you have time, ask one of your parents to read 1 Corinthians 15 with you and talk about the kind of love Christ offers us.

    c. Okay, I said I'd do this one. I think we can define fellowship by thinking of one of our friends. Think of your best friend. Think about how much fun it is to hang out together and talk and share things. That is *fellowship*!

We have fellowship in Christ because He is always there for us. He is always ready to hear us, to help us, to be on our side.

    d. I also promised to do this one, didn't I? Well, *affection* is what you feel for your best friend—you like him or her very, very much! You have affection for that person.

In Christ, there is an affection, a "liking" like you have for a friend. Just think that there is affection on top of love!

    e. Now for the last one. *Compassion* is what you feel for someone when you know he or she is are having a hard time. It is also a feeling of wanting to help that person with their trouble. Isn't it good news to think that you have compassion in Christ? The next time you are having a hard day, remember that He has compassion for you!

4. Now that we have defined these things you have in Christ, can you see why Paul would want you to walk worthy of them? They are great, great things to have! These are some of the most precious treasures in life, and we should show our appreciation for them!

5. Now that we understand what we have in Christ, let's begin to look at what Paul says about how "to walk in a manner worthy" of it all. Read Philippians 2:3-5 on your "Treasure Map" and look for four things we can do to walk worthy. I'll give you the first couple of words of each one to get you going.

- do nothing _____
- regard one another _____
- do not merely _____
- but _____
- have this _____

**We'll talk more tomorrow about this important thought—walking worthy!
See you then.**

LAYER TWO: Selfishness Is Out!

1. Yesterday we talked about what we have in Christ. We also began to understand how we could walk worthy of the gospel. We listed four things that Paul says we are to do if we want to walk this way.

Go back to the end of yesterday's lesson and look at them again. Then we will talk about these things.

2. When we are selfish, we only think of ourselves. When Paul talks about empty conceit, do you know what he means? It is sort of the same thing as being selfish.

Conceit means you think more of yourself than you should. When he says it is empty conceit, he means you are thinking of yourself in a way that you do not deserve.

Write out something you could do for your parents that would show that you do not want to be selfish.

3. How can we regard someone else as more important than ourselves? Think about what we talked about in number 2 above. What do you think?

Yes, we can act in a way that isn't selfish! And we can think of what another person likes or needs and do what they like or try to help meet his or her need.

4. Again, we see that we are not to look out for our own interests but for the interest of others. Their interest is what is best for them. Write down one way you can look out for someone else's interest instead of your own. Think about a brother, sister, or friend and write your thoughts.

5. Can you see that all of these things have to do with thinking of others and not yourself? It is sometimes hard to do that when you really want something special or when you think you're right! But isn't it great to understand that learning to think this way is a part of walking worthy?

6. The last way we discovered that we could walk worthy was to have the same attitude that Jesus had. Let's talk today about what that means.

a. If we are to have the same attitude as Jesus, we have to know what Jesus' attitude was. Turn to your "Treasure Map" and read Philippians 2:5-11.

b. Read back through Philippians 2:5-11 again and this time mark the word *Jesus* with a red cross. Also mark all pronouns that refer to Jesus, words like *He, His,* and *Himself*.

c. Today, let's make a list of all you have learned about Jesus from Philippians 2:5-11. The easiest way for you to do this is to go back and look at the words you marked with a cross. See what you learn about Jesus by looking to see what is said about Him each time you marked His name.

I'll put the heading down for you and get you started by numbering the list. List one by one what you learn about Jesus. You may need to add more numbers.

JESUS

1.

2.

3.

4.

5.

6.

7.

8.

9.

10.

Don't be concerned right now about understanding all of what you just listed. We'll keep talking about all that it means.

Do you know that Jesus is the greatest treasure you can seek? No other treasure can compare to knowing Him as your Savior, your Master, your Friend!

You've done really well. I am proud of you. Hang in there because this is a very important dig. See you tomorrow!

LAYER THREE: How's Your Attitude?

Let's talk more about what you've seen about Jesus. Remember we are trying to understand His attitude because Paul is telling us to have that same attitude. It is one of the ways we can walk worthy. Ready? Great! Let's go.

1. Look back over the list you made yesterday about Jesus.

2. Read Philippians 2:6 again and look at the two things you see. These two things were true of Jesus before He became a man. Note these two things. I'll help you a little.

Jesus e _____ in the f _____ of _____

Jesus did not regard e _____ with _____ a thing to be g _____

3. What does it mean to be equal? Can you explain it in a few words? **Clue #13:** Think about when your mom slices a pie. Don't you want the largest slice? Does she ever tell you they are all the same size? Okay, you try it now.

4. Do you know what it means to grasp something? **Clue #14:** Think about how a football player holds onto the ball as he runs down the field. He doesn't want to let go of it, does he? He wants to hang on to it and make the touchdown. He has a "grasp" on the ball, and he won't let go for anything.

So what does it mean to grasp something? Explain it in your own words now.

5. Philippians 2:7 tells us what Jesus had to do to become a man. List the three things you see.

e _____ Himself

took the form of a b _____ (Does that sound familiar???)

made in the l _____ of _____

6. Do you think what you listed in number 5 means that Jesus quit being God?

If you said no, you're right. Jesus has always been and always will be God. He decided to become man so that He could take care of our sin. Remember when we talked about Jesus dying and taking the keys away from the devil? He had to be a man to do that, and we'll talk more about that later.

God has three parts. God is the Father. Jesus as a man shows us another one of the parts of God. Do you remember when we talked about what the Holy Spirit is? Right, that's it! He is our teacher. He is the third part of God.

7. What position did Jesus fill when he became a man? Look in verse 7 to see. You listed it in number 3.

Do you remember what we talked about earlier when we talked about bond-servants? If you can't remember, go back to Dig Four and review what we discovered.

8. How did Jesus humble Himself?

by becoming _____

9. How obedient was He? Verse 8 says it was to a certain point—it tells how far He was willing to go to be obedient. To what point?

10. In verse 9, we see how God responded to Jesus' obedience? List the two ways God responded.

God highly e _____ Him

God bestowed on Him the _____ above _____ _____

11. One day every person who is alive or ever lived will respond to Jesus. What do you see in verses 10-11 about what will happen?

every _____ should _____

every _____ should _____ that _____ _____ is _____

12. So we see that Jesus was God. But because He loves you, He became man to pay for your sin. To become man, He had to do several things:

- He had to empty Himself.
- He had to become a bond-servant.
- He had to humble Himself.
- He had to be obedient.

It is pretty amazing to think about God becoming a man, isn't it? We'll keep talking about why He did that. But I think it is pretty awesome too that He was obedient to His Father while He was man.

Now don't you think if God as a man obeyed His Father that you, too, should always obey your parents? Even when you don't understand why they ask you to do something? I know your obedience will please God!

Think about all you've learned today as you get ready to take off for some fun now. See you soon.

LAYER FOUR: He Was a Humble Man

Yesterday we discovered that we are to have the same attitude that Christ had. We saw that He put aside His right to use His power as God for His own benefit. He emptied Himself—He gave up His right to be one thing (God) and became something else (man).

He also *humbled* Himself by becoming obedient. This means He lowered Himself from a place that was rightly His—to be God! Instead of ruling, He became a man and became obedient to God the Father.

The world doesn't understand the idea of not holding on to our rights or of being humble. Most people can't understand why you would choose to obey God rather than doing what you would want to do. Most people do not put others ahead of themselves. Let's look at some other scriptures that teach us about humility.

1. Read 1 Peter 5:6

Therefore humble yourselves under the mighty hand of God, that He may exalt you at the proper time.

a. Who is responsible for doing the humbling?

b. Who is responsible for exalting?

c. When does He exalt you? What does it mean? **Clue #15:** If being humble means to be willing to take a lower position or not to be the first, what would the opposite be?

2. We just read that God is responsible for exalting us. What happens to those who try to exalt themselves? Read Matthew 20:26-27.

> **26** …whoever wishes to become great among you shall be your servant,
> **27** and whoever wishes to be first among you shall be your slave.

a. Who are the truly great ones?

b. What does He say about those who try to be first?

Sometimes it's hard not to want to push ahead and be first, isn't it? It can be tough, too, when you see someone you think is wrong and you just want to tell them all about how to do it right—your way, that is!

Think about what you've learned today. Think about how you can be concerned for what the other person needs or wants. Think about not pushing yourself ahead or always wanting to be first. God will see your humility, and He will exalt you—or put you ahead—when He knows it is best!

We'll finish our digging for the week tomorrow. See you then.

LAYER FIVE: Jesus Paid for You

Remember a couple of days ago when we saw that God became man? He was called Jesus.

Do you remember that Jesus had to do several things to come to the earth as a man? Can you remember what they were? Let's review them. Look back to Layer Three, number 10 to see these listed.

As we continue to dig today, remember that He was obedient to the point of dying on a cross!

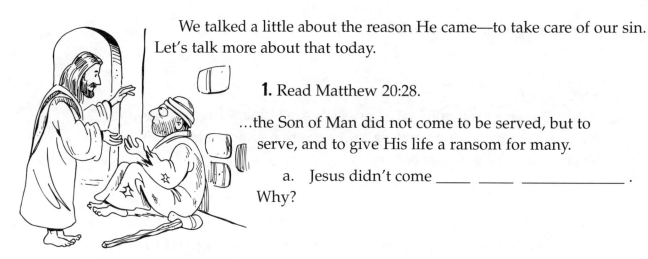

We talked a little about the reason He came—to take care of our sin. Let's talk more about that today.

1. Read Matthew 20:28.

...the Son of Man did not come to be served, but to serve, and to give His life a ransom for many.

   a. Jesus didn't come _____ _____ _____ .
Why?

b. Why did He come? There are two reasons. Write them both.

2. He came to serve. How did He serve you?

Right! He died for your sin!

3. He also came to be a ransom for many. To ransom means that you free something or someone by paying the price required by the one who is holding the person or thing. So let's talk about what ransom Jesus had to pay and why.

4. Do you remember when we talked earlier in Dig Four about the devil having the keys to a room you were locked in? Because the devil tempted Adam and Eve and they disobeyed God and gave in to him, he won and they became sinners.

And the devil won control over mankind. So the devil has the keys to the room of sin that you and all of mankind are locked in. The only way you could get out of that room is for someone else to take the keys away from the devil and open the door. And Jesus did that. Jesus paid the ransom that lets Him take the keys away. Let's see what the ransom was and how He paid it.

5. In order for Jesus to be able to take you back and ransom you from the devil, He had to be like you. He had to become a man. Read Hebrews 2:14-15.

> **14** Therefore, since the children share in flesh and blood, He Himself likewise also partook of the same, that through death He might render powerless him who had the power of death, that is, the devil, **15** and might free those who through fear of death were subject to slavery all their lives.

6. Because you are flesh and blood, He became the same—man.

7. You also see that the devil had the power of death. He had that power because Adam and Eve gave in to him and died in their spirits when they disobeyed God. A picture of that is his having you locked in the room of sin. As long as you are in that room, your spirit is dead. Read Romans 6:23.

> For the wages of sin is death, but the free gift of God is eternal life in Christ Jesus our Lord.

8. Do you understand that being a sinner means that you are dead in your spirit—in the part of you where God wants to live and make you alive?

Special Find: While we are here, let me tell you something else about the Holy Spirit. He is your Teacher, but He also has another very important job! The Holy Spirit comes to live in you in your spirit, when you ask Jesus to save you. That is how God lives in you! Through the Holy Spirit!

9. Let's look now at the price that Jesus paid for you. Let's see how He was able to take away the keys from the devil.

God set the ransom price. God decided what had to happen for you to be set free from sin and be forgiven. Read Hebrews 9:22.

> And according to the Law, … all things are cleansed with blood, and without the shedding of blood there is no forgiveness.

10. Blood had to be shed for you to be forgiven. Jesus loved you so much that He was willing to pay that price. Remember that you saw in Layer Two that Jesus was obedient even to death on a cross. This is why. He died to pay the ransom price for you!

11. Read John 3:16.

> For God so loved the world, that He gave His only begotten Son, that whoever believes in Him shall not perish, but have eternal life.

12. It was very, very painful for God to give up His Son to die on a cross. But He loved you so much too, and together with the Holy Spirit they put a plan in place to get you out of the room of sin.

13. Read Revelation 1:18 to see what Jesus says about the keys to the room of sin or death.

> [And He said, "I am] the living One; and I was dead, and behold I am alive forevermore, and I have the keys of death…."

14. Jesus died, and God raised Him from the dead. He won over death because He lived as a Man but He did not sin. He was obedient. [Remember we got into the room of sin because Adam and Eve were disobedient.]

Jesus took the keys of death, the keys to the room of sin. He opened the door. You can be free!

This is a most important study day. Be sure to talk all of this over with your mom or dad. If you haven't already, you can decide to accept the gift Jesus offers you. You can be FREE! It is the most important decision you'll ever make in your life.

I am proud of you. If you haven't alreadyyou have been a faithful digger this week, and you are to be commended. This Dig has contained some amazing treasures—ones that are super valuable!

I will see you in Dig Nine. Take a break and think about all you've discovered during this dig!

TRUTH TREASURES FOR THE WEEK

1.

2.

3.

BURY THE TREASURE:

…whoever wishes to become great among you shall be your servant, and whoever wishes to be first among you shall be your slave (Matthew 20:26-27).

Dig 9

Let Your Light Shine!

Tools of the Trade

1. Colored pencils
2. Pen or pencil
3. Treasure Map on the book of Philippians on pages 155-160
4. Bible

Directions for Diggers

You've come a long way in our dig on the book of Philippians, and you're storing up lots of treasures for life!

I'm proud of you!

This week we're going to explore Philippians 2:12-18 and take a very close look at the two things Paul tells the people in the city of Philippi to do.

Paul talks very honestly to them about obeying. He reminds them of how they obeyed while he was with them. And he wants them to obey just like that even though he is not there!

Have your mom and dad ever gone on a trip and left you with a babysitter for a couple of days? They told you to give the dog a bath before they got back. You decide to put it off until the night before they come home. Before you know it, they are back and you have forgotten!

Paul doesn't want his friends to live that way. He encourages them to obey. He doesn't want them to delay and be forgetful. He doesn't want them to get tangled up or distracted by things that aren't important. He wants them to obey just as if he were there telling them what to do and seeing them do it—in person!

So, let's go! Do you have all your gear? Are you ready to dig in? Have you checked in with headquarters? All right, let's hop in the jeep and head to the dig!

LAYER ONE: Who Lives Inside You?

1. First today, let's dig out an important verse. Read Romans 15:4 in your Bible and write it out below.

2. Do you see that what Paul wrote to these people in Philippi is also for you? Yes, Romans says that whatever was written in earlier times—what Paul wrote to the Philippians—was written for our instruction—for you and me—so we'd know how to live.

So now that we understand that all we are seeing and studying is for us today, let's dig into our verses for this week.

3. Let's begin our work in Philippians together by turning to your "Treasure Map" and reading Chapter 2:12-18.

4. Did you see the two things Paul told the people to do? Take another look and see if you can find these two instructions. **Clue #16:** Dig really hard in verses 12 and 14. Write below what Paul tells them in these verses. I'll get you started!

Verse 12: Work out _____ _____ with _____ and _____

Verse 14: Do all _____ without _____ or _____ (complaining)

First remember when we find a verse that is hard to understand we must stop and examine it a bit at a time. It's just like when an archaeologist finds bits and pieces of an old water jar or a table. He may have all of the pieces, but he has to patiently study each part and see how he can make each part fit together. Eventually he has a whole! You'll have a whole too—a total understanding—if we take time to look at each part and see how they all fit together. So let's start with the first of these two truths.

5. Let's look at what the first verse means when it says *work out your salvation*. We know that salvation is a gift, don't we? We talked about how

Jesus took the keys from the devil to set you free. Your job is to believe and to accept that gift of freedom.

So, if salvation is free, why does this verse say something about working? What do you think "work out" could mean? Take a shot at it if you can. If you don't have an idea what it means, go ahead and see what I think below.

I think *work out* is sort of like your mom asking you to be kind to your little sister because you love her. When we love someone, it means we should act a certain way toward them. If you really love your little sister, you won't let her run out into the street when a car is coming. You'll stop her. You "work out" your love.

I think Paul is saying if you have been saved, and if you love God, then work that out in your life. Make your life *look like* you love God because you do!

6. Now that you have the idea, write out one way *you* can *work out* your salvation.

7. Now let's see how Paul completes this thought by digging into verse 13. What do you see? Who is at work in you?

Why is God working in you? What does that mean? Any ideas?

God is working in you, and you are to work out your salvation. Amazing! He is asking you to do your part at the same time that He keeps doing His part in your life.

8. Let's talk a little more about verse 13 and think of it in a little different way. Think about your next-door neighbor. Would you walk into their house and take a bath, put on pajamas, and tuck yourself in bed for the night without an invitation? Why not?

Right, because it isn't your house. You are not the "landlord" or owner of that house. Your neighbor is! You may not get the point yet, but keep working, and you will.

9. Read 1 Corinthians 3:16.

> Do you not know that you are a temple of God and *that* the Spirit of God dwells in you?

Do you see that you are where God lives on this earth? What does this verse say you are?

10. God dwells in the "temple" of your body. He is the Landlord of your body. Did you know that you are God's house on the earth? Remember we talked about the Holy Spirit being one of the three parts of God? He is the part of God who lives in your spirit! Read John 14:16-17.

> **16** I will ask the Father, and He will give you another Helper, that He may be with you forever; **17** *that is* the Spirit of truth, whom the world cannot receive, because it does not see Him or know Him, *but* you know Him because He abides with you and will be in you.

11. Where will the Spirit live when He comes?

12. So God, the Holy Spirit, is living *in* you, and He wants your life to look like He lives there. He is working in you to make you more and more like His Son, and He wants you to let what He is doing inside come through on the outside. So He lives in you, works in you, and He wants you to *work out* what He is putting in you.

13. Read Romans 8:29 and write it out below.

14. Remember in Dig Six when we looked at Romans 8:28? Go back and look up this verse and read 8:28-29 so you can see these two verses together.

15. Remember in Dig 4 when we talked about how sin entered the world?
Well, if you think through Romans 8:29, you can understand that when you become a Christian, you change. You have the Holy Spirit living inside of you, and you are no longer dead in your spirit. You are alive in Christ! Pretty exciting!
Romans 8:29 tells us that as you grow up in God you'll become more and more like your big brother, Jesus. You'll be *conformed into His image*!

16. Let's look at another verse that will help us see why God wants you to work out your salvation. Read 2 Corinthians 3:2.

You are our letter, written in our hearts, known and read by all men.

17. Paul wrote this in a letter that he wrote to other friends. These friends lived in Corinth and were called Corinthians. What does Paul call them in this verse?

18. Paul is also using language to paint a picture. He wants them to think of themselves as a letter. Who does he say will read this letter?

19. Can you see that Paul is using this picture of being a letter everyone can read to tell them that they are examples to everyone they meet and live with?

So now can you see why God would want you to *work out* your salvation? You, too, are an example to everyone you meet, to everyone you go to school with, to your family! You can be a letter for God!

God wants you to look like He lives inside so that others will want to know Him. He wants to give His free gift of life to everyone. He wants to let everyone out of the room of sin.

Remember that just by the way you live you can tell others about Jesus and who He is!

LAYER TWO: A Light on a Hill

1. Today let's begin by looking at the second instruction Paul gives to the Philippians in 2:12-18. Go back to Layer One and see what you discovered in verse 14. That is Paul's second instruction.

2. We are to do things without what?

3. How many things are we to do in this way?

4. What does it mean to grumble or dispute? Maybe it will help you to use another word for disputing. Using the word complaining will help you understand what Paul was saying. So from this point on, let's use *complain* for *dispute*. Now write what you think.

Yes, it means you go ahead and do what you are supposed to do, but you fuss and fume about it the whole time. You say why you don't want to do it. Why you shouldn't have to. Why you wouldn't if you could get away without doing it! You talk about the person who is asking you to do it. You make everyone who can hear you miserable.

5. Write out three things that are hard for you to do without grumbling or complaining.

We need to remember that God tells us through Paul not to live like this! We are to do what is right without any words of complaint or grumbling. So the next time you want to complain about your chores or grumble about what is for dinner, think of this instruction and remember that God is talking to you through Paul's words to the Philippians. Let's see what else we can learn from Paul.

6. Paul goes on in the next verse to tell us why we're not to grumble or complain. Read Philippians 2:15 and then we'll dig our way through it together.

7. If you don't grumble and complain, you'll prove yourself to be children of God. Paul uses two words to describe what kind of children of God you'll be. What are the two words? Can you write them out? I'll help you.

B _____ and i _____ children of God

8. What do these words mean? **Clue #17:** Your mom has just baked fresh cookies. She tells you and all of your brothers and sisters not to touch the cookies she has baked. Next thing you know, six cookies are missing! Your mom notices that six cookies are missing, of course, and wants to know who ate the cookies. Your brother tells her that he didn't but that he thinks you did. Your mom turns and asks you if you ate the cookies. Are you innocent? Are you blameless? Okay, now take a shot at explaining blameless and innocent.

9. Well, if you didn't eat the cookies, you were innocent. You didn't commit the crime, and then you are also blameless because you did not eat the cookies (even though your brother blamed you). Remember, you can blame someone for something, but that does not mean they did it!

10. Paul is telling us to be innocent—not to do things that we aren't supposed to do. Then if we don't do wrong things, we'll be blameless!

11. Paul goes on and says that we are to be above reproach in the midst of a certain kind of people. When he says we are to be above reproach, he means that we should live in a way that no one will have any reason to blame us. He goes one step further with the idea of blameless. He wants us to live so that no one will *ever* have a reason to blame us.

Then he tells us that we are living in the midst of a certain kind of people. When he says *in the midst of*, he means they are all around us. What kind of people are they? Write down what Paul calls them.

12. Do you know what a crooked and perverse generation means? If you listen to your parents talk about some of the bad things they hear on the news or read in the paper, you probably hear them talking about people like this. They are people who do not obey the law. They can even be people who are mean and cruel to others in the way they talk or act. They are not godly people.

Then Paul says what you can be to these people. What is it?

13. Read Matthew 5:14-16.

> **14** "You are the light of the world. A city set on a hill cannot be hidden; **15** "nor does *anyone* light a lamp and put it under a basket, but on the lampstand, and it gives light to all who are in the house. **16** "Let your light shine before men in such a way that they may see your good works, and glorify your Father who is in heaven."

14. What does Jesus call you?

15. What does He say about a city on a hill?

16. What does He say that people do with a lamp? What don't they do?

17. Jesus is using the same kind of language Paul used when he called you a letter. Jesus is painting a picture with His words. You can imagine if a city were on a hill that everyone who lived down below would see it. That is what He wants you to be—a light that shines where everyone else can see it.

Can you imagine lighting a light and hiding it under a basket? Pretty pointless, huh?

God wants you to work out your salvation and shine like a light so that His life in you will be seen by everyone you meet. He doesn't want you to hide what He is doing in you! He wants you to light up your world!

18. Write out three ways you can shine and be an example to the boys and girls in your school or on your team or in your church. Remember what you learned about grumbling and complaining as you write these out.

Tomorrow we'll dig deeper into Philippians 2:16. The Master Digger, Paul, has a few more things to say. Hang in there, we begin on Layer Three tomorrow!

LAYER THREE: Lights in the World

Yesterday we talked about grumbling and complaining and about living in a way that would prove we were children of God.

As we talked about living like children of God, we talked about living in the midst of a crooked and perverse generation. Today let's look at Philippians 2:16 where Paul finishes this thought.

1. Read Philippians 2:14-16 again so that you can see the entire thought Paul is talking with them about.

2. You remember from yesterday that you are:
- not to grumble or complain
- so that you can prove you are children of God
- who are innocent and blameless in the midst of a crooked and perverse generation
- among whom you appear as lights in the world

Now let's find out how you can let your light shine!

3. Unscramble the first six words of verse 16 to see how you can let your light shine. This is how you are to do it!

DIGLNHO GTFA HET RDWO FO FELI

_____ _____ _____ _____ ____ _____

4. Yes, you hold fast the word of life so that you are a shining light! When you think of holding fast, do you think of hanging on to something? Me too. Like your dog hangs on to his favorite bone. But in this verse, the words mean to *hold out*. So we see you are to hold out the word of life. We are to offer it to others!

5. Do you know what the word of life is? Read John 6:68.

Simon Peter answered Him, "Lord, to whom shall we go? You have words of eternal life."

6. Who does Peter say has the words of life?

7. So we see that Jesus' words are the word of life. We can know, too, that all of the Bible is the word of life because God gave all of the words in both the Old and New Testaments. Jesus spoke some of them in person when He lived on the earth.

8. Now that we know what the word of life is, how can you *hold fast the word of life to a crooked and perverse generation*? Think about what we discussed when you uncovered the truth about working out your salvation. Think about being a shining light. Write what you think.

9. Yes, you can hold forth the word of life by letting God work in you and by living out what you know is true about Him every day! By shining His light wherever you are!

10. List three ways you want to hold forth the word of life this week.

We'll dig deeper tomorrow. Today, ask God to help you remember to hold forth the word of life as you go through the rest of your week.

LAYER FOUR: Tagging Your Finds

Today, let's practice a skill you began to develop a few weeks back. Let's make a list of some things we can unearth in Philippians 2:1-18 about how we can hold forth the word of life.

Today you'll tag our "finds" in these verses—just like archaeologists tag their treasures. These treasures tell us how to live so we can hold forth the word of life!

I'll give you the verse where you can unearth each treasure, and you write the find down in your own words.

Verse 3 Tag: Do nothing _____ conceit

Verse 4 Tag: Do not _____

_____ of others

Verse 5 Tag: Have this _____

_____

If you can't remember what you learned about these treasures when you unearthed them in Dig 8, go back and review your finds. Then write a summary of what you see in these verses about holding forth the word of life.

I'll see you tomorrow for our final day of digging this week as we tackle Layer Five. Today I am grateful for all your determination!

LAYER FIVE: Paul—Our Example

Today let's dig to the bottom of Layer Five and finish our discoveries for this week.

1. Read Philippians, chapters one and two on your "Treasure Map." As you read, take your green colored pencil and mark the name Paul with a large green "P." Also be sure to mark the pronouns that refer to Paul, words like *him, he, his.* Don't get discouraged, this won't take as long as you may think. It is hard digging, but I know you can do it!

2. Now go back and look at all of the times you marked Paul's name. See what you can find about how he held forth the word of life. Make a list of what you learn below. I'll start the list for you. You'll see that I put what I learned in my own words. You can do the same.

How Did Paul Hold Forth the Word of Life?

Verse 4: He prayed for the people he loved so that they would do well.

Verse 18: He rejoiced that Christ was being proclaimed even though it was because he was in prison.

Verse ___ :

Verse ___ :

Verse ___ :

Verse ___ :

Verse ___ :

Verse ___ :

Verse ___ :

Verse ___ :

3. Again, write a summary of what you've seen from Paul's life about holding forth the word of life.

It has been a great dig, hasn't it? You've worked really hard, and you've made it to the bottom of Layer Five!

Think back over what you have learned about being children of God and about being a good example. Think too of what you saw yesterday and today about holding forth the word of life. Then note your truth treasures for the week.

**Well, I'm off to see my friend.
Maybe you can do the same! You've earned it!**

TRUTH TREASURES FOR THE WEEK

1.

2.

3.

BURY THE TREASURE:

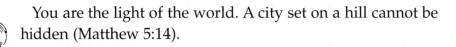

You are the light of the world. A city set on a hill cannot be hidden (Matthew 5:14).

Dig 10

To the Rubbish Pile!

Tools of the Trade

1. Colored pencils
2. Pen or pencil
3. Treasure Map on the book of Philippians on pages 155-160

Directions for Diggers

Ready for this dig? Good, me too!

This will be a time of digging for more treasures about the apostle Paul. You're going to learn more about the life he lived before he met Jesus and got out of the room of sin. And you'll get to see what the goal for his life was after Jesus set him free. Pretty exciting stuff!

Have you ever set a goal for yourself? Have you ever decided to make a B in a subject instead of a C? Have you tried to jump higher on the basketball court than you did last season? Have you ever told yourself you couldn't have ice cream until you finished your homework? These are all goals.

It is important to set goals because they make us work hard, concentrate, and focus. You'll see that Paul set a goal for his life. And because he set his sights on that goal, some things that would distract him had to go!

Don't forget to check in with headquarters. That is vital! Then we'll be off to the dig!

LAYER ONE: True Followers

1. Today we'll dig into a new chapter of Philippians—chapter 3. Find this chapter on your "Treasure Map" and read verses 3:1-3.

2. First you see Paul encouraging these people to rejoice in the Lord. We talked in Dig Six about rejoicing. We know that even though Paul was in prison he was rejoicing because more and more people were hearing about Jesus.

3. Paul also reminds them of some things they have talked about before. He says that he knows being reminded of truth will help keep them safe. Let's see what Paul says they need to remember.

4. Paul warns the Philippians of three things in verse 2. As we start our study today, let's list those three things and talk a little about each one. As usual, I'll get you started. Read verse 2 again and fill in the blanks.

3 Things Paul Warns About

1 Beware of _____ _____

2 Beware of _____ _____ _____

3 Beware of _____ _____ _____

5. Paul's warning is against three groups of people. What do you think about calling people *dogs*? (Don't laugh!) Paul is saying that some of the people who live in this city are *acting* like dogs because they are fighting like dogs over what to believe and not believe.

The second group are people who were not doing the will of God. They were even going so far that they did evil things—they were *evil doers*.

The third group is called the *false circumcision*. That's a tough one! Paul is talking about people who say they are righteous just because they are Jewish. It is true that the Jews are God's chosen people. Because they tried to keep the Law of the Old Testament, they thought they were holy. Obeying the Law was how the Jews thought they could please God.

When Jesus came, He brought a new plan that took the place of keeping the Law to please God. Jesus said the Jewish people would now have to obey Him. Some of these Jewish people could not let go of the Law and follow Jesus. They did not understand that He came to replace the Law. They were afraid to change the way they had always done things. Paul calls these people the "false circumcision."

6. Paul warns the Philippians not to get involved with any of these groups. He wants them to work out their salvation, just as we learned in the last chapter. So now he is warning them that these groups could distract them and keep this from happening.

As you read the rest of the chapter today, you'll see that Paul's goal was to know Christ and then to make Him known to others. He wanted them to know and follow Jesus too.

Paul did not want them to be distracted from the most important goal. He did not want them to bother arguing with people who were not following Jesus. That could keep them from the goal.

Are there things that could get in your way of doing what God wants you to do? Sometimes would you rather watch television than work on your Bible study? It isn't that television is all bad, but we need to be careful not to let it get in the way of something more important!

What are some things that could keep you from learning about Jesus? What could distract you? List the things you can think of.

7. Now let's look at Philippians 3:3 again and see what Paul says we are. Read the verse again on your "Treasure Map."

8. You see he says the Philippians are the "true circumcision." Remember God is also talking to you through this letter, so you're a part of this group too!

Let's see what we can learn about this group. Read verse 3 again and look for three things you see about them. Write those below.

The True Circumcision

1

2

3

Can you see that these people want to please Jesus? They *worship* in the Spirit of God. This means they *focus* on Jesus and the Father and are *grateful* for all they have done for them. They *glorify* Jesus by obeying Him. And they *put no confidence in the flesh*. In other words, they know they need to trust Jesus and not themselves.

9. If Jesus has set you free from the room of sin, He paid a price for you. You are His. Remember in Dig Nine that we talked about God being like a landlord? If you are a Christian, the Holy Spirit lives in you, and you are to let God work in you to make you like Jesus. You are a part of the "true circumcision!"

As God works in you, you'll begin to look more and more like one of His kids. Remember that you are to let what He works in you come out. Then everyone else gets to see what Jesus looks like!

You've dug up lots for one day! Sift back through all that you have
uncovered and be sure you understand it. Then put your feet up!
You've done a good day's work. See you tomorrow!

LAYER TWO: Where Is Your Confidence?

Yesterday, you saw that you're a part of a group of people Paul calls the "true circumcision." What was the last thing he said was true of that group? Look back and see, and we'll talk about it today.

1. Paul says those who are a part of the true circumcision *put no confidence in the flesh.* Do you know what confidence is? Write what you think it is.

2. If you have confidence, it means you know you can do it. You are certain. You are sure. You have no doubt. Paul says we are not to have confidence in our flesh.

When he talks about flesh here, he means our humanity. He means who we are without Jesus. Some of you may be really good students. You may be able to remember things really well. You may be able to read and understand all you have read. BUT Paul says that you should not put your confidence in your own ability.

Your confidence is to be in Jesus. You should remember if you are a good student that Jesus gave you your brain. If you will rely on Him and ask Him, He will help you use it wisely. You may have an ability, but it is from Him!

3. Paul goes on and says that he can understand that it may be hard not to trust your abilities. He says he has lots of reasons to trust his flesh. He lists those reasons. See if you can find them in Philippians 3:5-6. Let's do this together.

1 _____ the eighth day

2 of the nation of _____

3 of the tribe of _____

4 a _____ of the _____

5 as to the Law, a _____

6 as to zeal, a _____ of the church

7 as to the righteousness which is in the Law, found _____

There were things the Jewish people were to do in the Old Testament to stay in right standing with God. Remember we just talked about how the Old Testament Jews were to keep the Law in order to stay in fellowship with God? That was before Jesus replaced the Law! Paul was a Jew, and he did *ALL* he was supposed to do according to the Law. He was very proud of himself.

So can you see that Paul is saying that he was a very good Jew? Paul had done everything he was supposed to do as a Jew. And he did it very well. He had every reason to think that he was just fine. If you only looked at Paul's life from the outside, you'd think he was perfect. It didn't look like he needed Jesus to save him—because he obeyed the Law.

But that is not the end of the story! Tomorrow we'll see what else Paul says. Hang in there. You're learning lots!

LAYER THREE: Running for the Goal

1. Read Philippians 3:7-11 as we begin today.

2. Instead of putting confidence in his flesh, what did Paul do? Read verse 7 again to be sure you don't miss this!

3. In verse 8, Paul tells us that he counted all things loss for the "surpassing value" of something else. Surpassing value means it is so valuable that nothing else could be worth as much as it was! What was it that he valued so much? Write it out below.

4. What else does Paul say in verse 8 about those things that would have held him back from knowing Christ. He says he counts those things as what?

5. If he says all of these things were like rubbish—garbage—to him, does he think they were important?

6. When Paul compared the things that were important to him to knowing Christ, he decided they were like rubbish! No one hangs on to their garbage, do they? It is pretty powerful way to tell us how he feels!

7. Now stop and read Philippians 3:12-14.

8. Paul is pressing on toward his goal. What is his goal? (Read verse 10 again to see how he states his goal.)

9. Paul says that he hasn't gotten to the goal yet, but he sure wants to, doesn't he? What is the one thing he says he is doing in verses 13-14?

10. Paul wants to know Christ! He says he is forgetting what is behind. When he says that, he is saying that even though he was a good Hebrew—Jew—he is letting go of that so he can know Christ. He understands that Jesus replaced the Law. Now he wants to know this Jesus! Everything else is like rubbish! It is all worthless to him now that he has a true life goal. Only the things that help him reach the goal matter.

11. But what else do you know about Paul's past? Think back to Dig Two and review what you learned about him in Acts. Write a short summary of what you see.

12. Paul was a good Jew, but he was also a hater of Christians. To know Christ, Paul had to let go of the good things he did as a Jew and of the bad things he did to the church. He had to go forward. Paul did not want to be distracted from his goal.

He knew if he held on to his past—the good or the bad—that he would get off track. Have you ever watched the Olympics and seen men and women running races? They line up for the race, bend over, put their hand at the starting line, and look straight at the goal.

Then when the gun goes off to start the race, they run toward the goal. They do not look back to see where the other runners are. They don't pull out the record book from the last race to see how they did. They don't stop to visit with one another, to get a soda pop, or to make a phone call. None of those things will help them get to the goal. They run hard and straight toward the goal!

Paul knew he had to focus on his goal—Jesus. Paul wanted to know Jesus, and he wanted to live in a way that would let other people see Jesus in him. He wanted to make Jesus known. He knew he could not look back.

Remember that if you do not know Jesus now, you can know Him from this point on. Whenever you come to Him and ask Him to let you out of the room of sin, you can then have a new goal of *knowing* Jesus.

There will never be a greater treasure to cherish than knowing Him!

LAYER FOUR: Your Life Goal

Yesterday we saw why Paul had a good reason to put confidence in his flesh. And you also saw why he decided not to! Today let's talk about you.

1. List some of the reason you could put confidence in your flesh. Think about your abilities, your family background, your skills. Make a list of at least five things that you could be proud of or have confidence in. I'll use one of mine to get you started.

- I am really good at math.

-
-
-
-
-
-
-

2. Now I know you are not in high school or college, so you may not know yet what you will do when you finish school. But think for a few moments about goals. Think about Paul's goal for this life. What are some of your goals right now in your life? List at least three.

-
-
-

Good! It's great to have some goals. They will probably change as you get older, but you should always have goals you are working toward.

3. Paul did not want to be distracted from his goal. He wanted to run in a way that allowed him to win. Think about the Olympic runners again. Have you ever seen a runner in combat boots? No, you see him in the best running shoes he can afford! He doesn't want anything to keep him from winning the race. That's how Paul felt.

Think about how his goal made him let go of things that didn't help him reach the goal. Paul didn't keep things around that would take his attention off of his goal! He didn't try to run toward his goal in combat boots!

Are there things that may keep you from your goals? What should you do about them?

4. Think about what you might want for your life goal when you grow up. Talk to your mom and dad about goals and about your thoughts on your life goal. Ask them to talk with you about what you would need to do to get to that goal. Write out what you think your goal could be.

5. What kinds of things could keep you from your life goal? What are you willing to do about those things? Are you willing to start your own rubbish pile?

6. Remember, as we started this week's dig, we talked about three groups of people who Paul thought could be distracting to the Philippians. Paul loved these people, and he wanted to be sure that they reached their goal of being like Jesus. Sometimes other people can see things that can hold you back because you can't see them. Talk with your mom and dad about things they may see that could hold you back. Ask them to help you think about how to avoid those things.

**Lots to think about, huh? Give your brain a rest.
See you when we break through Layer Five tomorrow!**

LAYER FIVE: Follow Me

One last day of digging for the week. You've worked so hard, and I know you'll always treasure the truths you've discovered this week. These truths can really help you all through your life as you set goals.

BUT the greatest truth you have unearthed is that Paul understood that his past, his good works, his wisdom, his standing in the community, his knowledge—nothing—was as important as knowing Jesus and making Him known to other people.

Paul was so convinced that he was on track that he told the Philippians to follow his example.

1. Look at this verse for yourself. Read 3:17.

2. Does Paul tell them to watch how anyone else is living? Who?

3. Paul tells them to watch others who are living like he lives. He is telling them that he is a good example and that others who live the same way are too. How was Paul living that would let him say this? Think back to what he says about counting everything as loss. What was Paul's one desire in life?

That's right, he wanted to know Christ. And he wanted others to know Him too. He counted everything else as rubbish when He compared it to knowing Christ.

4. Let's jump ahead to chapter 4 and see another time when Paul tells them that they can follow him. Read 4:9.

5. Write out below what Paul tells them they can practice.

The things you have   **1**

                     2

                     3

                     4

Pretty amazing to be living in such a way that you know you can tell someone else to follow your example, isn't it? Are you living like Paul?

Do you want to know Christ? Do you want God to work in you? Do you want to live in a way that others can look at you and see Jesus?

Are you a shining light? Are you living out what God is working in you? Are you willing to put things that would keep you from knowing Christ on the rubbish pile?

Talk to your mom and dad about all you have uncovered in these last two digs. The truths you have found are **BIG** ones, and you may want to make some very important decisions in light of them.

I am proud of you. I know that even if you can't sort through all of the treasures you have found and decide what to do with them right now that one day you'll know. I pray that day comes soon.

You are a great digger! Don't forget your Truth Treasures!
Then take a nice break and rest up for the next dig!

TRUTH TREASURES FOR THE WEEK

1.

2.

3.

BURY THE TREASURE:

...I count all things to be loss in view of the surpassing value of knowing Christ Jesus my Lord, for whom I have suffered the loss of all things, and count them rubbish so that I may gain Christ (Philippians 3:8).

Dig 11

Your Thoughts Matter...

Tools of the Trade

1. Colored pencils
2. Pen or pencil
3. Treasure Map of the book of Philippians on pages 155-160
4. Bible
5. Missing Pieces Puzzle on page 139

Directions for Diggers

Can you believe that this week we will start to dig in the last part of Paul's letter to the Philippians?

This last chapter of the book of Philippians is the conclusion to all that Paul has been saying to the Philippians. In it, he says some things he wants to be sure they won't forget. He also sends a special personal message to two women there. Then he thanks the Philippians for some money they have sent to help him.

The last chapter is a lot like the end of a letter you'd write to a good friend. You'd throw in some important thoughts you may have forgotten earlier, and you'd say good-bye to your friend and thank him for caring about you.

**This week we'll dig in the first part of the chapter,
and in Dig Twelve we'll examine the last part. Let's look at Paul's conclusion!**

129

LAYER ONE: Rejoice I Say!

Over these last ten weeks of digging in this book, you've seen that Paul loved the believers in Philippi very much. As he ends his letter, he gives them some instructions that he says will help them live in the peace of God. Let's see what he says.

1. Turn to your "Treasure Map" and read Philippians 4:1-8.

2. Now go back and see if you can find the instructions given in these verses. **Clue #18:** Dig around especially hard in verses 1, 5, and 6.

I'll get you started on these four instructions.

1 _____ _____ in the Lord

2 _____ ____ _____ _____ always

3 ____ _____ _____ _____ ____ _____ to all men

4 _____ _____ for nothing _____ ____ _____

___ _____ _____ _____ ___ _____ ___

_____ _____ ____ _____ known to God

3. Today let's look at the first two instructions to see what we can learn for our lives. In verse 1, Paul tells the Philippians to *stand firm in the Lord*. Write what you think it means to *stand firm*.

4. Yes, if you stand firm, you don't sway back and forth. You don't wish-wash. You stay in the same place. So if you stand firm in the Lord, how would you act? Think about what you have learned about working out your salvation and about being a light in the world.

Yes, you would act like you know Him and live for Him no matter what. You don't get shaken by what is happening or by what people say. You know what you believe, and you keep on believing it and acting like you believe it in every circumstance and in every group of people! This is for sure how Paul wanted these people to live—and it is certainly how we are to live!

5. Look up 1 Corinthians 16:13 and copy it below. Remember that you saw in Dig Nine that Paul had friends in a city called Corinth and that he wrote letters to them too. This is another verse from his first letter to those people.

6. Again, we see Paul tell these people to *stand firm.* What else does he say here about standing firm?

7. Do you think *standing firm in the faith* is the same as *standing firm in the Lord*? Why?

8. I think it is the same. If we are in the Lord, we are there because we had the faith to ask Him to save us from sin. Faith means believing in something you cannot see and touch. Do you have faith in the Lord?

9. We talked in Dig Six about rejoicing. Do you remember how Paul talked about rejoicing—even though he was in prison—because the gospel was spreading? Paul brings the subject up again. Let's look at all the times that Paul talks about rejoicing in this book and see what we can learn.

I'll give you each reference. You find it on your "Treasure Map" and read it. As you read, take your yellow pencil and put a big smiley face over the word *rejoice.*

- **Philippians 1:18** Paul is talking about Christ being preached more because he is in prison. He rejoices!

- **Philippians 2:17** Paul is saying that even though he is "being poured out" he rejoices. He means that even if his life is being used up so that they have faith, he is happy.

- **Philippians 2:18** In light of what he says in verse 17, he encourages them to rejoice.

- **Philippians 2:28** He is talking about a man, Epaphroditus, who is a friend to them also and who has been sick. Epaphroditus is going to visit them, and Paul knows they will rejoice—be happy—to see him.

- **Philippians 3:1** Paul says finally, rejoice in the Lord. I think he is saying to them that because of all he has told them, they should rejoice. They should be glad that Paul is encouraging them and giving them truth.

- **Philippians 4:4** Paul tells them to rejoice. Here, it is one of the final instructions he is giving to those he loves.

10. Look up Proverbs 17:22 and write it below.

11. What did you learn in Proverbs about a joyful heart?

12. What does medicine do when you are sick?

You've seen that a joyful heart—a heart that rejoices—is like medicine. Medicine helps you feel better, and a joyful heart makes your spirit feel better!

13. You see from the beginning of his letter to the end, Paul talks about rejoicing. It is one of the things he repeats again and again. Paul rejoices because he knows God, and he knows He is in control. He wants the Philippians to learn to have that kind of confidence too—and to rejoice. And God wants you to have a joyful heart, a heart that rejoices because you know He is in control and will work all things out for your good!

Can you stand firm in the Lord and rejoice today because you know God and because you trust Him to work all things together for your good? If you can't, talk to God about it. If you can, tell God that you want Him to teach you more about being joyful!

LAYER TWO: No More Worries

Today let's look at the next two instructions Paul gives and see what we can learn for our lives.

1. Go back to Layer One and read Paul's third instruction.

2. If you have a *gentle spirit*, how do you think you would act?

Sometimes I think people get the wrong idea of what gentle is. I think they think it is being sissy or weak. But if you have a gentle spirit, you aren't hard to get along with. You are kind to everyone—whether they are your favorite person or not!

Paul tells us here that we are to be aware of how we are acting. We are to make every effort to be kind and agreeable—to have a gentle spirit. Other people will see Jesus when we display a gentle spirit.

As you let what God is doing in you come out—as you work out your salvation—this kind of spirit will become more and more a part of you!

Can you think of someone who has a gentle spirit? Would you like to be like them? Why?

3. Let's look at another time when Paul tells the Corinthians something like this. Read and then write out 1 Corinthians 16:14.

4. If you act and react out of a heart of love, your gentle spirit will shine through! Think about how you have acted toward your brother, sister, or friend in the last couple of days. Would they think you have a gentle spirit?

5. Now go back to Layer One and read the fourth instruction. It's a little long, but we'll get through it pretty fast, so don't be concerned!

6. When things aren't going your way, what do you do? When you have a big test and you aren't sure how you'll do on it, what do you do? When you have a piano recital or a ballet recital, what do you do? When you have a big game and you're up against the best team, what do you do? Do you ever worry?

Well, this instruction tells us to *be anxious for nothing*. Not to worry. Can you think of why Paul can say this? Think back over all you have learned and write what you think. Think of Joseph!

Yes, you remember, don't you, that God is in control. Even when we can't see how He is at work, we know that He is.

7. This instruction goes on and tells us what to do instead of being anxious—or worrying. What does it say?

We're to talk to God about the things that concern us! We must remember that He is in control, that He loves us, and that He cares about all that we think, feel, and fear.

We are to pray, and in the prayer we are to give thanks. What can you be thankful for? Well, for starters you can always be thankful that He is in control!

As you start, do you know what the word supplication means? Paul tells them to make their requests known in prayer and supplication with thanksgiving.

Supplication means special prayers for specific things. Like praying for your friend who is sick. Or praying for your sister to do well on her test she has studied so hard for. So be specific in your prayers!

Write a prayer and thank Him. Be thankful that you don't have any reason to worry. Also, if there is anything you need to ask for specifically, include that supplication in your prayer.

Tomorrow, we'll talk about the result of living in light of these four instructions!

LAYER THREE: Amazing Peace!

1. Today start by reading Philippians 4:7. What is the result of living in a way that you follow Paul's instructions?

2. What is the peace of God? Write what you think it is.

If you follow these instructions, you'll be living in a way that you are at peace with God and with others. You are standing firm, rejoicing, being kind to others, not worrying but praying. You have peace in your heart because you know the King of the Universe—He is your heavenly Father—and you're living in a way that pleases Him!

3. Can you explain what Paul means when he talks about the peace of God that *surpasses all comprehension*? Comprehension means how much you can think about and understand. **Clue #19:** Have you ever "surpassed" the last grade you made on an English test? If you have, it means you got a better score.

Yes, he means it is so peaceful that you cannot imagine it! You can't comprehend it! You can't grasp it! It goes too far beyond the peace we can understand to be able to get it!

Today think of the kind of life you can live—a peaceful one! And ask God to remind you of this the next time something happens that you would usually worry about. Or the next time you get angry at your brother, sister, friend, or parent and don't want to be gentle or loving.

Tomorrow we'll look at the thoughts we are to fill our minds with so that we don't worry. See you then!

LAYER FOUR: Great Things to Think About

After talking for a moment about the peace of God in verse 7, Paul gives two more instructions in verses 8 and 9. Today let's look at those.

Let's begin by talking about a way we can think that will guard our minds and that will let us live without worry!

1. Today begin by reading Philippians 4:8.

2. Paul now gives us help in knowing how we can think so that we are not distracted by our thoughts. So that we can live the life he is challenging us to live. Go back and look at verse 8 again and list what he tells us to think about.

WHATEVER is...

-
-
-
-
-
-

3. Let's see if you can match the things Paul tells us to think about with their opposite meanings. I'll list the words that describe how we are to think in the column on the left. On the right, I'll scramble the opposite meanings. Put the letter of the opposite meaning in the blank beside the correct word.

___ **True**		**A. Not Trustworthy**
___ **Honorable**		**B. Wrong**
___ **Right**		**C. Ugly**
___ **Pure**		**D. Dishonorable**
___ **Lovely**		**E. Not clean**
___ **Good Repute (well thought of)**		**F. A lie**

4. Do you see what you are *not* to think about? The opposites are those things you shouldn't think about!

5. In this verse, you see the word *if* used two times. Both times, the word means *because*. Go back and read the verse again and substitute the word *because* for the two *ifs*.

6. Do you see that Paul is telling us that the things he tells us to think about are excellent and worthy of praise? We know that anything that fits into one of the two categories is a *GOOD* thing to think about!

7. Paul tells us to dwell on these things. Can you define dwell in the way Paul uses it here? **Clue #20:** Have you ever wanted to go to a certain movie and you ask and ask if you can go and your parents haven't answered you yet? You ask again, and your dad finally says," Let's not dwell on that"?

If we dwell on something, aren't we always thinking about it?

Well, if we'll let our minds dwell on—always be thinking about—things that are true, honorable, right, pure, lovely, of good repute, we won't be anxious and we'll have thoughts that please God! Is it worth a try? I sure think so!

LAYER FIVE: Take Care of How You Think

Yesterday we saw how to think so that we don't worry. Today let's talk more about why we should think correctly.

1. Read Proverbs 4:23 and copy it below.

2. When the word *heart* is used in the Bible, sometimes you can substitute the word *mind* for it. The verse you just read is one of those places. Write the verse again and substitute *mind* for *heart*.

3. Your mind is where you think and reason. What you think about will affect how you act. So you see that the springs of life—the way you act or your behavior—flows out of your heart (or mind).

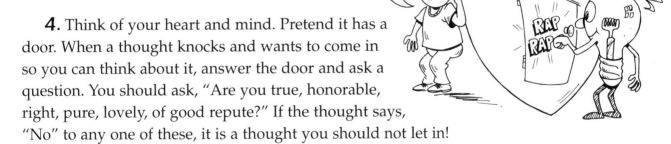

4. Think of your heart and mind. Pretend it has a door. When a thought knocks and wants to come in so you can think about it, answer the door and ask a question. You should ask, "Are you true, honorable, right, pure, lovely, of good repute?" If the thought says, "No" to any one of these, it is a thought you should not let in!

5. Now read the first half of Proverbs 23:7 and write it below.

6. Again you see that however a man thinks, he is. So what you think about affects how you act!

7. Can you see why you need to think correctly? Decide today what you want to do about how you think. Tell God about it by writing out a short prayer.

8. Now let's take a quick look at Paul's last instruction to the Philippians. It is in verse 9. Read it.

9. Do you remember that we talked about this verse in Dig Nine when Paul talked about following his example? Now we see the verse with everything around it he was saying as he ended his letter.

Paul wants these people to do well. He wants them to be strong in the Lord. He knows they can look at his life and see how to live so that they do well. (Notice that he again mentions the God of peace!)

Do you want to live in a way that will let you tell others to follow you? It is a worthy goal! And if you are living to know Christ and to make Him known, you'll be able to say it to others!

Well, it has been a full week of digging. But you have seen some key truths in Paul's instructions—treasures that will help you build a strong life in Christ! Think about all you've learned and record your Truth Treasures.

You'll see a fun puzzle on page 139, so work that and then take a break. Next week will be our last dig in the book of Philippians, so rest up!

TRUTH TREASURES FOR THE WEEK

1.

2.

3.

BURY THE TREASURE:

Be anxious for nothing, but in everything by prayer and supplication with thanksgiving let your requests be made known to God (Philippians 4:6).

MISSING PIECES PUZZLE

There are 17 letters of the alphabet missing from this puzzle. They are listed below. See if you can find where they belong in order to complete the puzzle. Cross each letter off as you find its place. When you finish the puzzle, you'll see that these are all words from this week's dig!

A B C D E G H I L N R T U V W W X Y

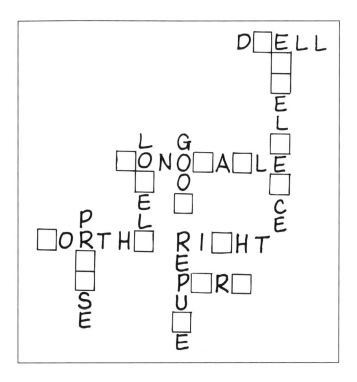

Dig 12

Treasures of Truth

Tools of the Trade

1. Colored pencils
2. Pen or pencil
3. Dictionary
4. Versigram on page 147.

Directions for Diggers

Believe it or not, this is our last dig in the book of Philippians!
We'll spend this time looking at the end of chapter 4 and reviewing what you have discovered in these last eleven weeks.

Ready to head off. Let's go!

LAYER ONE: A Contented Person

1. Today we will begin where we left off last week—with Philippians 4:11-13. Read these verses, and then we'll talk through it.

2. Paul says he has learned to be content in whatever situation he finds himself. Look up the word for content in a dictionary and write it below.

3. Paul says he has learned to live in humble means—with very little. He says he also knows what it is like to live in prosperity—with a lot of things. What does he say about how he has learned to live in either situation—whether he is living with a lot or a little?

4. What is the secret? Paul tells us in verse 13.

5. Again, we see that Paul knows God is in control, and he trusts Him. So Paul can be content —happy—with what he has because he knows God sees all that is happening, knows every detail of what is happening, and is taking care of him in the middle of what is happening.

He says he can do all things through Christ—he can be content and live in any situation because of what he knows about God and about Jesus.

6. Read Hebrews 13:5-6.

> **5** Make sure that your character is free from the love of money, being content with what you have; for He Himself has said, "I will never desert you, nor will I ever forsake you," **6** so that we confidently say, "The Lord is my Helper, I will not be afraid. What will man do to me?"

7. What do you see in these verses about being content?

8. From what you read here, what is the main reason we can be content?

Don't you want to learn to be content no matter what? If you come to a point where you believe that God is in control and that He wants what is best for you, you will be content! Remember He has said that He will never leave you or forsake you!

Thank God today for loving you, for caring for you, for sending His Son to die for your sins. If you truly want to learn to be content in all things, tell Him.

LAYER TWO: Sharing Our Money

1. Let's keep reading through chapter 4 of Philippians. Read 4:14-18.

2. What is Paul thanking them for?

Paul talks about how grateful he is that they have shared with him. Even though he knows how to live without a lot, he is thankful that they would care for him by sending him money.

3. In verse 17, Paul says that he is not so interested in the gift but in the *profit which increases to your account*. Can you figure out what he means by this? I think he is saying that he is so thankful that they would want to give money to be a part of the work God has asked him to do. They were helping Paul spread the gospel with their gifts.

Paul says it increases to their account. I think this means that God will reward the people for helping Paul and for being a part of sharing the gospel in this way.

4. Do you go to a church that gives money to people who work in other countries teaching people about God? If your church helps missionaries—people whose job is to teach others about Jesus—you could ask your mom and dad to let you help by giving some of your allowance each month.

If your church doesn't help missionaries in this way, and you are interested, ask your mom and dad to help you find a way to help a missionary.

LAYER THREE: Our Good Shepherd

1. Today let's look at Philippians 4:19. Read the verse, and then we'll talk about it.

2. Paul shares a great treasure with these people in verse 19. Write the verse out below.

3. Paul knows firsthand that God takes care of our needs. He was encouraging these people by telling them what he had learned about God. How many of their needs did Paul say God would meet?

4. Read Psalm 23:1 and write it out below.

5. What is the Lord called in Psalm 23:1?

A good shepherd never lets his sheep need anything. Again we see words painting a picture for us. If the Lord is our shepherd, He will care for us like a shepherd cares for his sheep.

6. What do you see about your need in Psalm 23:1? (The word want in this verse is used in a way that means *have a need*.)

Thank the Lord, the Good Shepherd, today that He will take care of all your needs. Thank Him too that He will never leave you or forsake you!

Isn't it exciting to know that you can be content with what you have? Isn't it encouraging to know that God will take care of your needs? This truth may not mean that you get all you want, but you'll get what you NEED!

LAYER FOUR: A Treasure Chest of Truth

You've made it! You have dug your way through the entire book of Philippians! And I know you have stored away some amazing treasures for life. Think back through each lesson and write out below one truth you'll always treasure! Don't panic. Look back in each lesson if you need to refresh your memory.

Truth Treasures from the Book of Philippians!

1

2

3

4

5

6

7

8

9

10

11

12

There is a Versigram on page 147. It is a bit of a mind-bender, but it'll be great fun and a good review of the book of Philippians. Start on it today.

Thank God for all He has taught you in these weeks.
Don't forget to show up for Layer Five tomorrow!

LAYER FIVE: Things to Remember Forever

As you dig to the bottom of the last layer of your study in Philippians, take about ten minutes and write a couple of paragraphs about the neatest treasure you discovered.

Now take the time to share what you have written with you teacher, a friend, your parents, or a grandparent.

If you didn't finish the puzzle yesterday, work to finish it today.

You have done an amazing job! You've crossed the goal line of Philippians. I cannot tell you how proud I am of you! I know that these truths you have mined will be treasured all the days of your life. And I know you will grow up to be a great man or woman of God if you will live in the light of them.

BURY THE TREASURE:

...I have learned to be content in whatever circumstances I am (Philippians 4:11).

VERSIGRAM

Unscramble these important verses from Philippians. I'll tell you what chapter to look in if you need help.

1. oFr em, ot vile si riChst nad ot eid si niag.

_____ (Chapter 1)

2. nOly ductcon serlvouyes ni a annmer thorwy fo eht spelgo fo hrtsiC.

_____ (Chapter 1)

3. oD lla gsniht othtiwu nbgurilmg ro ptingusid.

_____ (Chapter 2)

4. nFiayll, ym rerenthb, jiocere ni hte orLd.

_____ (Chapter 3)

5. eB axsiuon rof thnigno.

_____ (Chapter 4)

6. I nac od lal gtihns thhrgou iHm hwo gthstreensn em.

_____ (Chapter 4)

Key to Games

People Puzzle on page 16

Hidden Names

(P)   A   U   L

C   (L)   E   M   E   N   T

E   U   O   D   (I)   A

E   (P)   A   (P)   H   R   O   D   I   T   U   S

T   (I)   M   O   T   (H)   Y

S   Y   (N)   T   Y   C   H   E

B   E   N   J   A   M   (I)   N

C   (A)   E   (S)   A   R

New Scramble Name

(P)   (L)   (I)   (P)   (P)   (I)   (H)   (N)   (I)   (A)   (S)

P   H   I   L   I   P   P   I   A   N   S

Key Word Puzzle on page 30

1 L I G H T

2 D A M A S C U S

3 S A U L

4 V I S I O N

5 T A R S U S

6 I S R A E L

7 B A <u>P</u> T I Z E D

8 <u>C</u> H U R C H

Key Word

2	1	5	8	4	7	3	6
D	I	S	C	I	P	L	E

Word Dig Crossword Puzzle on page 44

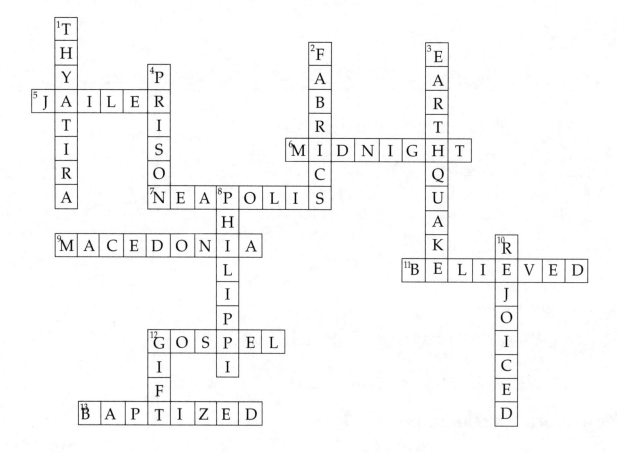

Answers to map on page 45

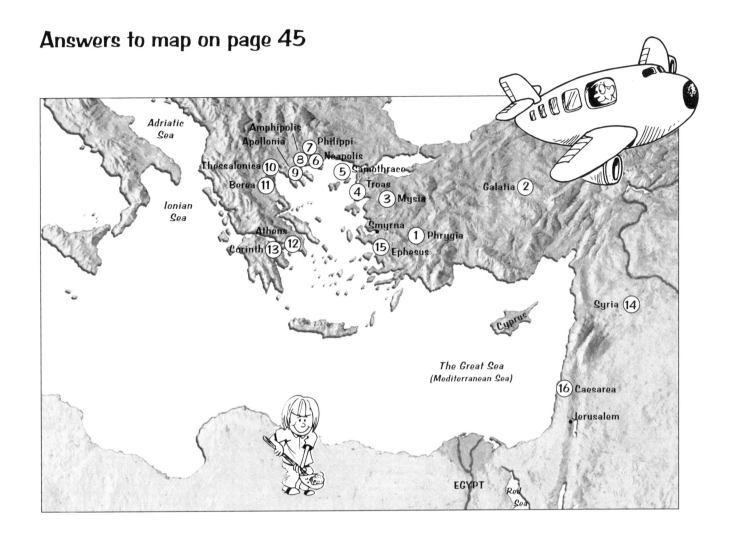

1.	Phrygia	**9.**	Apollonia
2.	Galatia	**10.**	Thessalonica
3.	Mysia	**11.**	Berea
4.	Troas	**12.**	Athens
5.	Samothrace	**13.**	Corinth
6.	Neapolis	**14.**	Syria
7.	Philippi	**15.**	Ephesus
8.	Amphipolis	**16.**	Caesarea

Seeking Saints on page 56

S	A	I	N	T	S	S	A	I	N	T	S	A	S	T
I	T	S	A	I	N	T	S	N	T	A	N	A	S	
S	S	I	S	A	I	N	T	S	T	I	S	A	A	
S	A	I	N	T	S	T	T	A	N	N	A	I	I	
S	I	S	N	A	N	S	S	I	T	T	I	T	N	
S	N	A	T	N	S	A	I	N	T	S	N	S	T	
A	T	I	S	S	A	I	N	T	S	A	T	S	S	
I	S	N	S	S	I	N	N	S	A	I	S	T	A	
N	A	T	S	T	N	T	A	N	T	N	A	A	T	
T	I	S	S	T	T	S	S	S	T	I	A	N	N	
S	N	N	N	S	S	A	I	N	T	S	N	I	T	
S	T	S	A	I	N	T	S	T	S	A	T	N	S	
S	S	A	I	N	T	S	A	I	N	T	S	T	S	
T	T	S	S	T	T	S	S	S	A	A	T	S	T	

Word Search on page 68

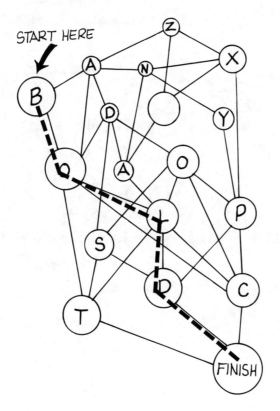

START HERE

Z
A N X
B
D Y
Q A O
P
Y
S D C
T FINISH

Key Word Puzzle on page 94

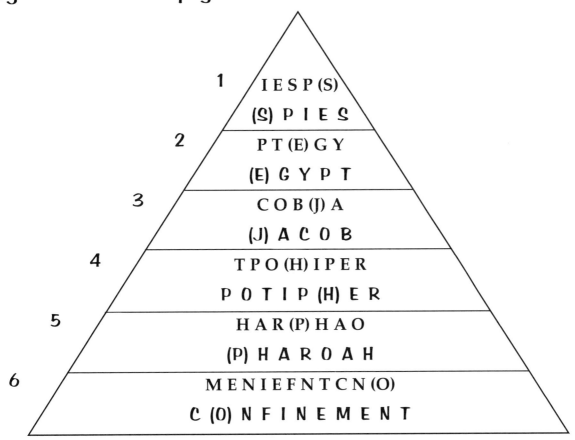

1 I E S P (S)
   (S) P I E S

2 P T (E) G Y
   (E) G Y P T

3 C O B (J) A
   (J) A C O B

4 T P O (H) I P E R
   P O T I P (H) E R

5 H A R (P) H A O
   (P) H A R O A H

6 M E N I E F N T C N (O)
   C (O) N F I N E M E N T

NEW NAME SCRAMBLE

(S) (E) (J) (H) (P) (O)

J   O   S   E   P   H

Missing Pieces on page 139

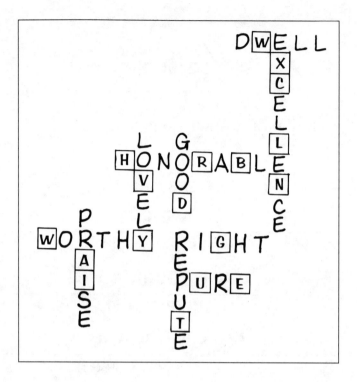

Versigram on page 147

1. For me, to live is Christ and to die is gain.

2. Only conduct yourselves in a manner worthy of the gospel of Christ.

3. Do all things without grumbling or comlaining.

4. Finally, my brethren, rejoice in the Lord.

5. Be anxious for nothing.

6. I can do all things through Him who strengthens me.

Treasure Map
of the book of Philippians

Chapter 1

1 Paul and Timothy, bond-servants of Christ Jesus, to all the saints in Christ Jesus who are in Philippi, including the overseers and deacons:

2 Grace to you and peace from God our Father and the Lord Jesus Christ.

3 I thank my God in all my remembrance of you,

4 always offering prayer with joy in my every prayer for you all,

5 in view of your participation in the gospel from the first day until now.

6 *For I am** confident of this very thing, that He who began a good work in you will perfect it until the day of Christ Jesus.

7 For it is only right for me to feel this way about you all, because I have you in my heart, since both in my imprisonment and in the defense and confirmation of the gospel, you all are partakers of grace with me.

8 For God is my witness, how I long for you all with the affection of Christ Jesus.

9 And this I pray, that your love may abound still more and more in real knowledge and all discernment,

10 so that you may approve the things that are excellent, in order to be sincere and blameless until the day of Christ;

11 having been filled with the fruit of righteousness which *comes* through Jesus Christ, to the glory and praise of God.

12 Now I want you to know, brethren, that my circumstances have turned out for the greater progress of the gospel,

13 so that my imprisonment in *the cause of* Christ has become well known throughout the whole praetorian guard and to everyone else,

14 and that most of the brethren, trusting in the Lord because of my imprisonment, have far more courage to speak the word of God without fear.

15 Some, to be sure, are preaching Christ even from envy and strife, but some also from good will;

16 the latter *do it* out of love, knowing that I am appointed for the defense of the gospel;

---

* Italics are used in the text by the translators to indicate words not found in the original Hebrew, Aramaic, or Greek but implied by it.

17 the former proclaim Christ out of selfish ambition rather than from pure motives, thinking to cause me distress in my imprisonment.

18 What then? Only that in every way, whether in pretense or in truth, Christ is proclaimed; and in this I rejoice, yes, and I will rejoice.

19 For I know that this will turn out for my deliverance through your prayers and the provision of the Spirit of Jesus Christ,

20 according to my earnest expectation and hope, that I will not be put to shame in anything, but *that* with all boldness, Christ will even now, as always, be exalted in my body, whether by life or by death.

21 For to me, to live is Christ and to die is gain.

22 But if *I am* to live *on* in the flesh, this *will mean* fruitful labor for me; and I do not know which to choose.

23 But I am hard-pressed from both *directions*, having the desire to depart and be with Christ, for *that* is very much better;

24 yet to remain on in the flesh is more necessary for your sake.

25 Convinced of this, I know that I will remain and continue with you all for your progress and joy in the faith,

26 so that your proud confidence in me may abound in Christ Jesus through my coming to you again.

27 Only conduct yourselves in a manner worthy of the gospel of Christ, so that whether I come and see you or remain absent, I will hear of you that you are standing firm in one spirit, with one mind striving together for the faith of the gospel;

28 in no way alarmed by *your* opponents—which is a sign of destruction for them, but of salvation for you, and that *too*, from God.

29 For to you it has been granted for Christ's sake, not only to believe in Him, but also to suffer for His sake,

30 experiencing the same conflict which you saw in me, and now hear to be in me.

Chapter 2

1 Therefore if there is any encouragement in Christ, if there is any consolation of love, if there is any fellowship of the Spirit, if any affection and compassion,

2 make my joy complete by being of the same mind, maintaining the same love, united in spirit, intent on one purpose.

3 Do nothing from selfishness or empty conceit, but with humility of mind regard one another as more important than yourselves;

4 do not *merely* look out for your own personal interests, but also for the interests of others.

5 Have this attitude in yourselves which was also in Christ Jesus,

6 who, although He existed in the form of God, did not regard equality with God a thing to be grasped,

7 but emptied Himself, taking the form of a bond-servant, *and* being made in the likeness of men.

8 Being found in appearance as a man, He humbled Himself by becoming obedient to the point of death, even death on a cross.

9 For this reason also, God highly exalted Him, and bestowed on Him the name which is above every name,

10 so that at the name of Jesus EVERY KNEE WILL BOW, of those who are in heaven and on earth and under the earth,

11 and that every tongue will confess that Jesus Christ is Lord, to the glory of God the Father.

12 So then, my beloved, just as you have always obeyed, not as in my presence only, but now much more in my absence, work out your salvation with fear and trembling;

13 for it is God who is at work in you, both to will and to work for *His* good pleasure.

14 Do all things without grumbling or disputing;

15 so that you will prove yourselves to be blameless and innocent, children of God above reproach in the midst of a crooked and perverse generation, among whom you appear as lights in the world,

16 holding fast the word of life, so that in the day of Christ I will have reason to glory because I did not run in vain nor toil in vain.

17 But even if I am being poured out as a drink offering upon the sacrifice and service of your faith, I rejoice and share my joy with you all.

18 You too, *I urge you*, rejoice in the same way and share your joy with me.

19 But I hope in the Lord Jesus to send Timothy to you shortly, so that I also may be encouraged when I learn of your condition.

20 For I have no one *else* of kindred spirit who will genuinely be concerned for your welfare.

21 For they all seek after their own interests, not those of Christ Jesus.

22 But you know of his proven worth, that he served with me in the furtherance of the gospel like a child *serving* his father.

23 Therefore I hope to send him immediately, as soon as I see how things *go* with me;

24 and I trust in the Lord that I myself also will be coming shortly.

25 But I thought it necessary to send to you Epaphroditus, my brother and fellow worker and fellow soldier, who is also your messenger and minister to my need;

26 because he was longing for you all and was distressed because you had heard that he was sick.

27 For indeed he was sick to the point of death, but God had mercy on him, and not on him only but also on me, so that I would not have sorrow upon sorrow.

28 Therefore I have sent him all the more eagerly so that when you see him again you may rejoice and I may be less concerned *about you.*

29 Receive him then in the Lord with all joy, and hold men like him in high regard;

30 because he came close to death for the work of Christ, risking his life to complete what was deficient in your service to me.

Chapter 3

1 Finally, my brethren, rejoice in the Lord. To write the same things *again* is no trouble to me, and it is a safeguard for you.

2 Beware of the dogs, beware of the evil workers, beware of the false circumcision;

3 for we are the *true* circumcision, who worship in the Spirit of God and glory in Christ Jesus and put no confidence in the flesh,

4 although I myself might have confidence even in the flesh. If anyone else has a mind to put confidence in the flesh, I far more:

5 circumcised the eighth day, of the nation of Israel, of the tribe of Benjamin, a Hebrew of Hebrews; as to the Law, a Pharisee;

6 as to zeal, a persecutor of the church; as to the righteousness which is in the Law, found blameless.

7 But whatever things were gain to me, those things I have counted as loss for the sake of Christ.

8 More than that, I count all things to be loss in view of the surpassing value of knowing Christ Jesus my Lord, for whom I have suffered the loss of all things, and count them but rubbish so that I may gain Christ,

9 and may be found in Him, not having a righteousness of my own derived from *the* Law, but that which is through faith in Christ, the righteousness which *comes* from God on the basis of faith,

10 that I may know Him and the power of His resurrection and the fellowship of His sufferings, being conformed to His death;

11 in order that I may attain to the resurrection from the dead.

12 Not that I have already obtained it or have already become perfect, but I press on so that I may lay hold of that for which also I was laid hold of by Christ Jesus.

13 Brethren, I do not regard myself as having laid hold of *it* yet; but one thing *I do*: forgetting what *lies* behind and reaching forward to what *lies* ahead,

14 I press on toward the goal for the prize of the upward call of God in Christ Jesus.

15 Let us therefore, as many as are perfect, have this attitude; and if in anything you have a different attitude, God will reveal that also to you;

16 however, let us keep living by that same *standard* to which we have attained.

17 Brethren, join in following my example, and observe those who walk according to the pattern you have in us.

18 For many walk, of whom I often told you, and now tell you even weeping, *that they are* enemies of the cross of Christ,

19 whose end is destruction, whose god is *their* appetite, and *whose* glory is in their shame, who set their minds on earthly things.

20 For our citizenship is in heaven, from which also we eagerly wait for a Savior, the Lord Jesus Christ;

21 who will transform the body of our humble state into conformity with the body of His glory, by the exertion of the power that He has even to subject all things to Himself.

Chapter 4

1 Therefore, my beloved brethren whom I long to *see*, my joy and crown, in this way stand firm in the Lord, my beloved.

2 I urge Euodia and I urge Syntyche to live in harmony in the Lord.

3 Indeed, true companion, I ask you also to help these women who have shared my struggle in *the cause of* the gospel, together with Clement also and the rest of my fellow workers, whose names are in the book of life.

4 Rejoice in the Lord always; again I will say, rejoice!

5 Let your gentle *spirit* be known to all men. The Lord is near.

6 Be anxious for nothing, but in everything by prayer and supplication with thanksgiving let your requests be made known to God.

7 And the peace of God, which surpasses all comprehension, will guard your hearts and your minds in Christ Jesus.

8 Finally, brethren, whatever is true, whatever is honorable, whatever is right, whatever is pure, whatever is lovely, whatever is of good repute, if there is any excellence and if anything worthy of praise, dwell on these things.

9 The things you have learned and received and heard and seen in me, practice these things, and the God of peace will be with you.

10 But I rejoiced in the Lord greatly, that now at last you have revived your concern for me; indeed, you were concerned *before*, but you lacked opportunity.

11 Not that I speak from want, for I have learned to be content in whatever circumstances I am.

12 I know how to get along with humble means, and I also know how to live in prosperity; in any and every circumstance I have learned the secret of being filled and going hungry, both of having abundance and suffering need.

13 I can do all things through Him who strengthens me.

14 Nevertheless, you have done well to share *with me* in my affliction.

15 You yourselves also know, Philippians, that at the first preaching of the gospel, after I left Macedonia, no church shared with me in the matter of giving and receiving but you alone;

16 for even in Thessalonica you sent *a gift* more than once for my needs.

17 Not that I seek the gift itself, but I seek for the profit which increases to your account.

18 But I have received everything in full and have an abundance; I am amply supplied, having received from Epaphroditus what you have sent, a fragrant aroma, an acceptable sacrifice, well-pleasing to God.

19 And my God will supply all your needs according to His riches in glory in Christ Jesus.

20 Now to our God and Father *be* the glory forever and ever. Amen.

21 Greet every saint in Christ Jesus. The brethren who are with me greet you.

22 All the saints greet you, especially those of Caesar's household.

23 The grace of the Lord Jesus Christ be with your spirit.